MAKING PEACE IN THE GLOBAL VILLAGE

BOOKS BY ROBERT MCAFEE BROWN
Published by The Westminster Press

Making Peace in the Global Village

Theology in a New Key:
   Responding to Liberation Themes

Is Faith Obsolete?

Religion and Violence:
   A Primer for White Americans

The Pseudonyms of God

The Collect'd Writings of St. Hereticus

The Hereticus Papers
   (Vol. II of The Collect'd Writings of St. Hereticus)

The Significance of the Church
   (Layman's Theological Library)

The Bible Speaks to You

P. T. Forsyth:
   Prophet for Today

MAKING PEACE
IN THE
GLOBAL VILLAGE

by

Robert McAfee Brown

THE WESTMINSTER PRESS
Philadelphia

BOOK DESIGN BY DOROTHY ALDEN SMITH

First edition

Published by The Westminster Press®
Philadelphia, Pennsylvania

PRINTED IN THE UNITED STATES OF AMERICA
9 8 7 6 5 4 3 2 1

Library of Congress Cataloging in Publication Data

Brown, Robert McAfee, 1920–
    Making peace in the global village.

    1. Peace. 2. Peace—Moral and religious
aspects. 1. Title.
JF1952.B755   261.8'73   80–27213
ISBN 0–664–24343–6

To Pepo

CONTENTS

Continued

ACKNOWLEDGMENTS

Much of the material that follows originated in talks given over the last few years to groups concerned with peacemaking. I have tried to maintain the informal tone of such occasions in the transposition from the spoken to the written word. The Questions for Discussion grow out of memories of such occasions.

Portions of the material that have appeared in print before are as follows: A brief version of Chapter 1, "From Good News to Bad News to Good News," appeared in *A.D.* magazine in Feb. 1980 and is reprinted by permission. The first half of Chapter 2, "Modern Warfare: Challenge to Peacemakers," is adapted from my book *Religion and Violence* (Westminster Press, 1973), while the last half is adapted from an article in *Christianity and Crisis,* May 14, 1973, copyright © 1973 by Christianity and Crisis, Inc., and is reprinted by permission. Chapter 3, "Reversing the Arms Race," first appeared in Jane Rockman (ed.), *Peace in Search of Makers* (Judson Press, 1979) and appeared in brief form in *Maryknoll* magazine, Aug. 1979, and is reprinted by permission of Judson Press. Chapter 4, "To the Poor, Violence Is an Empty Stomach," contains excerpts from articles in the *Los Angeles Times* and *Ramparts* magazine, while Chapter 6, "Seeing America in Global Terms," was originally published in a special anniversary issue of the *St. Louis Post-Dispatch*, March 25, 1979, and is reprinted by permission. Chapter 5, "Christian Responsibility in Human Rights," and Chapter 7, "The Remnant Within the Remnant," appear in print for the first time, although a few fugitive paragraphs from them and from the initial essay made their way into my *Theology in a New Key* (Westminster Press, 1978).

I am grateful to Joyce Stoltzfus for a number of editorial suggestions and to Valerie Besenbruch for most of the typing.

Since this is a small book, readers who wish elaboration on some of the themes treated below can find more extended comments in my *Frontiers for the Church Today* (Oxford University Press, 1973), *Religion and Violence* (Westminster Press, 1973), *Theology in a New Key* (Westminster Press, 1978), and *Creative Dislocation—The Movement of Grace* (Abingdon Press, 1980).

INTRODUCTION

I am writing within five miles of one of the first nuclear power plants built after World War II. When it was opened, we all hailed it. "Atoms for peace," was the cry. How glad we were that atomic power—with such devastating possibilities for destruction—was being harnessed for creative ends. We had tamed the beast.

Today we know that the beast may yet have the last word. At present the plant is closed, due to a sequence of near-disasters. While there has been no Three Mile Island in this tiny corner of Vermont and Massachusetts, we know that such a catastrophe could occur here too. Real estate purchases in the town where the plant is located have plummeted almost to zero. Who wants to live next to a potential source of lethal destruction?

That's a tiny picture. But, writ large, it exemplifies the fact that our world today is a world full of unexpected consequences. Atomic energy was going to save us; it may destroy us. Increased armaments were going to ensure that we were "safe" from attack; they now make attack more likely, leaving us more vulnerable than before we had them. American "aid" to underdeveloped nations was going to gain us friends and a stable world; it now fertilizes a seedbed for enemies and new alignments of power. Re-

ducing tensions between East and West was going to remove reasons for global conflict; it now makes future conflict between North and South more likely. Greater prosperity for our people at home was going to "trickle down"
to benefit less fortunate folk elsewhere; it now spawns
greater gaps between the rich and the poor than were
there before.

Nothing is going according to plan. We seem to have
misread all the signs. The one thing of which we can be
✓ certain is that nothing is certain.

In such a precarious situation, it is important to take
stock. If the overriding issue is peace, we need to reflect
on some new ways of making peace, since we haven't been
notably successful in our attempts to do so in the past.
What this small book tries to do is to provide a *perspective*
for peacemaking, though not a *program*. It examines how
we have to look at our world—and ourselves—if we are to
be peacemakers. When we have done some grappling
with that, we will be in a better position to work on programs, which will become the order of the day as soon as
the book is closed. Such a perspective won't come out of
the blue, or out of heaven, or out of books, or out of abstract reflection. It will only come out of looking very
openly and honestly at the world we are in and what we
are doing within it. That is the stuff out of which a perspective—or a theology—comes.

There emerges a very simple starting point about which
Christians and non-Christians can agree. Juan Luis
Segundo, a Jesuit from Uruguay, has captured it: "The
✳ world should not be the way it is." Anybody who disagrees
can stop reading immediately. Nothing that follows will
make any sense.

So there are some long, hard looks at our world and at
ourselves in these pages. We must be prepared for the fact

that most of what we see won't seem reassuring or flattering. But unless we want to live in a fool's paradise (in today's world, "hell" might be a better word), we'd better start with the fact that (*a*) the view of the world *isn't* reassuring, and that (*b*) we North Americans aren't particularly well liked by the other inhabitants of that world. Anybody who has as much power as we have (whether military, political, economic, or covert) is bound to be viewed with suspicion. And anybody who throws power around the way we have done (whether in Vietnam or Chile or the Dominican Republic) is bound to be viewed with fear.

That being so, there are some questions we'd better explore at least briefly, if we intend to be serious about peacemaking in such a world. We will concentrate on three:

1. What *is* the nature of peacemaking anyway?
2. How does peacemaking relate to the other things we do?
3. With what kind of interpretive lens will we view the world around us?

1. What is peacemaking? On the face of it, nothing sounds more innocuous than an exhortation to peacemaking. Who isn't for peace? Who prefers war? But it all depends on what we mean by peace. Confronted with the demand for a spontaneous gut-level definition, most people initially respond, "Peace is the absence of war." That is surely part of it, and part of what we must do in the pages that follow is to measure the nature of modern war so we'll know what needs to be avoided. But the end, or absence, of war doesn't necessarily mean peace. Not for the wounded, the homeless, the orphans, the displaced

persons—those whose homes, factories, fields, and families are gone.

In Hebrew, the word for peace is *shalom,* and it is helpful in moving toward a more adequate understanding, for it suggests many positive things as well, some of them surprising. Without going into a long word study, we can establish that *shalom* in the Hebrew Scriptures means such things as wholeness and health, prosperity and security, political and spiritual well-being. It is often related to the notion of covenant, the bond or agreement between God and God's people, and the Messiah who comes to fulfill the covenant is frequently called "the Prince of *Shalom.*" So *shalom* indicates liberation, God's act of setting free, and it promises blessing as one of the possibilities for human life. *Shalom,* in other words, is much more than the absence of war, and it is much more than "inner" serenity, which is how Christians often try to spiritualize it. By contrast, true *shalom* is almost shockingly materialistic: it has to do with the state of one's belly, whether it is full or empty, whether it is a source of health or disease; it has to do with having adequate shelter; it has to do with a security that is physical as well as spiritual. It is very earthy. So concern for *shalom,* or peacemaking, doesn't just involve keeping us out of war (though it obviously includes that); it also involves seeing to it that people have enough to eat; that they are not undernourished or malnourished; that they can go to bed at night without fear that someone will spirit them off to prison; that the society will be so planned that there is food enough to go around; that the politics of the country (and of the world) are so arranged that everybody's basic needs are met. Otherwise, no *shalom.* There's still plenty of work to keep peacemakers busy.

2. This already elicits our second question: How does

peacemaking relate to the other things we do? The answer is clear: everything relates to everything else. Peacemaking isn't something we ought to do in our spare time, it's something we need to do all the time. Action to alleviate world hunger (including that down the block) is peacemaking; seeking to reverse the arms race is peacemaking; action on behalf of human rights is peacemaking; working for an economic order that narrows the disparities between rich and poor is peacemaking. Whatever enhances the well-being of the human family is peacemaking, the spreading of *shalom.*

How do we draw a bead on such a target? Pope John XXIII and Reinhold Niebuhr (perhaps the most eminent Catholic and Protestant, respectively, in our era) shared at least this in common: they believed that *the path to peace is found in the struggle for justice.* And that is something they both got from the Jewish Scriptures.

Justice. I want to suggest later that justice is seeing to it that each child has what is his or her due. On those terms, the definition of a just society, and thus of a peaceful world, and maybe, therefore, of the Kingdom of God, would go something like this: a place where the only privileged ones are the children. So we need to measure our world, and the imperative for peacemaking, with an eye to justice. Whatever is unjust threatens peace. Whatever fosters justice is an act of peacemaking.

Such an expansion of the agenda may seem overwhelming: too much to do. But it is meant to empower rather than immobilize. For whereas peacemaking in general may seem so vast as to be unattainable, relating peace to justice opens the door to every individual and every group to let peacemaking be part of what is done every day and in every way. Of course we cannot "do everything," but we can do one thing at least: engage in the struggle for human rights, or combat local instances of racism, or put heat on our congressional representatives to decrease military spending. Whatever it is, it can be *our* contribution to peacemaking, the point where we zero in, get a focus, acquire some expertise, and roll up our sleeves.

3. But there is another question: Is there a viewpoint from which we can make more rather than less sense of the apparent chaos around us? A new answer has gradually been emerging for me over the last few years. I guess I used to think that the *real* source of what jeopardized peace was located within our own hearts: our individual pride, self-centeredness, and occasional plain cussedness accounted for why things were askew. I haven't surrendered that to a counterassumption that people are really altruistic at the core and only selfish because they don't know any better. My disillusionment with the old answer isn't so much that it's wrong, but that it's inadequate. It doesn't explain enough. It doesn't explain the way *social structures* can be instruments of evil. It doesn't recognize that a lot of individually "good" people can collectively unleash a lot of evil (individually good bishops can perpetuate a sexist church, individually good businessmen can participate in decisions that throw thousands out of work, individually good faculty members can create structures that intimidate younger faculty, individually good scientists can together design weapons that maim persons but don't harm buildings). It doesn't acknowledge that people who really want to change things may be powerless to do so, because the outfits they work for (the corporation, the university, the army, the church) are dedicated to resisting change.

In the current discussion this reality is sometimes called "systemic" or "corporate" or "structural" evil. It is a way of acknowledging that even with the best will in the world we can get locked into structures that control us even when we think we are controlling them. No American corporation executive, for example, says to himself, "Let's see now: how can I devise a way to increase profits that will make children starve to death?" And yet, abhorring the notion of children starving to death, he may be forced to institute a company policy in a Third World nation (refusing to let workers bargain collectively, for example) that will have precisely the result that because of labor conditions in the country children *do* starve to death. He doesn't even have to institute the policy; acquiescence will be enough.

This is an uncomfortable avenue down which to be asked to walk in fidelity to concern for peacemaking, and yet I believe we must take the initial step and see what happens. For this is, in fact, how much of the rest of the world perceives people like those who read and write books like this. We want to do good—and evil results. Conclusion: What's good for General Motors may or may not be good for the country, but what's good for the country is clearly not good for the world. It is not good for the world if we, who are 6 percent of the world's population, continue to consume 40 percent of the world's resources. More significant conclusion: It is not good for us either, and when we learn that, peacemaking can begin in earnest.

Throughout these chapters, an attempt is made to acknowledge the evil that is present in our corporate structures as well as in our individual hearts. Dealing with systemic evil is not, of course, enough, and T. S. Eliot was right to warn us of the fallacy of "dreaming of systems so perfect that no one will need to be good." But changing individual hearts isn't enough either. If hearts have to change, so do structures. If a condition for peace is that individuals stop being so ravenously competitive, we can't ask them to survive creatively in an economic system that is. If individuals need a world in which the number of lethal weapons is reduced, we can't reach that goal as long as huge structures like corporations, the Pentagon, and the Armed Forces can dictate a national budget in which arms expenditures increase each year rather than decrease. If the rich are getting richer and the poor are getting poorer, and we think that's unjust but can't seem to change the direction, then we've got to ask: what structures in our society perpetuate a pattern of escalating injustice, and how can those structures be challenged?

These are far-reaching questions. It will take more than one small book to clarify them, let alone respond to them. But at the end of the process we might see more clearly that Paul wasn't talking first-century cosmology or outworn demonology when he talked about "principalities and powers" that were more than just individual aberrations and had some kind of independent power of their own. He was describing our world. And locating the enemy is half the struggle.

Each chapter that follows is complete in itself. But taken together, these chapters will, I hope, illustrate some sense of the interconnectedness for which this introduction has been pleading, since getting our own bearings is the other half of the struggle.

ROBERT MCAFEE BROWN

Heath, Massachusetts
Thirty-fifth anniversary of the bombing of Nagasaki

I | *Peacemaking in the Global Village*

1
FROM GOOD NEWS TO BAD NEWS
TO GOOD NEWS

At the height of the United States involvement in Southeast Asia in the 1960's, a group of morally outraged citizens managed to secure an appointment with Henry Kissinger, one of the chief architects and proponents of our policy. As the conversation became heated and the citizens were asking for the withdrawal of our troops, Kissinger challenged them on the complexities of such a withdrawal, asking (no doubt rhetorically), "How would *you* get the boys out of Vietnam?" William Sloane Coffin, then chaplain at Yale University and prominent in antiwar protest, was not one to let an opportunity slip by, rhetorical or not. He responded: "Mr. Kissinger, our job is to proclaim that 'justice must roll down like waters, and righteousness like a mighty stream.' Your job, Mr. Kissinger, is to work out the details of the irrigation system."

Putting aside the question of whether Coffin really wanted to give Kissinger carte blanche with the details, there is an important truth in the response. It is that Christians do not, just by being Christians, have any inside track on the *specifics* of political action or peacemaking. Prayer and piety do not by themselves produce good politics. Indeed, some of those who pray most in public often appear to have the worst politics. Christians have to do their

19

homework, listen to the experts, and learn from them, just like everyone else. But, if and when they have done that, they have a right to ride herd on what goes on in public life, to challenge policies that clearly contravene justice, and to demand policies that will make the social order less exploitive, less racist, less destructive, and consequently more conducive to peacemaking. It is a long, hard road from "the love commandment" to knowing just what social structures can best approximate that love, let alone discovering how to create such structures when those presently in power seem determined to maintain an unjust status quo at all costs.

How does one even begin to get leverage on the immensity of change that is needed if the global village is to be a realm of peace, creative and habitable for all its members? If Christians cannot by themselves work out all the details, they can at least be among those who will set the context for such an endeavor. This suggests a theme worth exploring: *It is the task of peacemaking Christians to insist that we think and act as citizens of the global village.* That may sound like bare bones as a starter; perhaps it can have some flesh, and even some teeth, before we are finished.

Is it good news or bad news that we have to live as citizens of the global village? I suggest that it is both. Let us start with the good news as a context for the bad news, after which we may be able to look once again at the good news, both realistically and hopefully.

The good news, of course, is that we don't have to search frantically for a place to start building the global village. That is already a given. It is provided by the community, the church, of which we are a part. The church at its best is not a parochial, regional, class, or national community.

It is itself already a foretaste of the global village, with members from every race and class and nation. It proclaims a God who is not the God of the few, or even the God of the many, but the God of all. There is no way such a God can be claimed as the privileged possession of whites or Americans or Republicans or males. I believe that this God makes what the Latin American bishops at Puebla called "a preferential option for the poor," and that we are therefore required to do likewise. But such an option is finally for the sake of *all,* so that as the rich are no longer able to exploit the poor, those who were formerly "rich" and "poor" can in the end become sisters and brothers.

So there is a wide-based human solidarity in the vision of the Christian faith. Minimally, it is the solidarity of *sinners,* all of whom have sinned and come short of the glory of God, and there is plenty of empirical evidence that that is a category from which no one is exempt (with one important exception). Maximally, it is the solidarity of *forgiven* sinners, a category from which no one is excluded, unless by his or her own choosing. The good news is that we are already one, no matter how we try to hide or corrupt that fact.

Our word "gospel" is a contraction of the early Anglo-Saxon *god spell* (good tale), often interpreted as "God's spiel," or "what God says." It is our unique counterpart of *euangelion/evangelium,* "good news." When we remember that in the Biblical perspective "word" and "deed" cannot be separated, and that what God *says* is what God *does,* and that God's "Word" is not a statement but an embodied life in Jesus of Nazareth, we really have quite a lot of good news to build upon. We are promised that God is to be found in the midst of our concrete, human experience—in a life lived, a death died, a grave overcome

—rather than in some abstraction or some far-off corner of the cosmos. If God is in the very stuff of our human existence, then *that* is where we must seek to find God, since that is where God is already seeking to find us.

So the good news is that this is the faith we affirm with our lips.

The bad news is that this is the faith we deny with our lives.

We are in a curious position: the truer the good news is, the worse off we are. To deny a hypothesis is not so bad; if the hypothesis does not conform to reality, we are better off denying it. But to deny something that turns out to be descriptive of the way things actually are—that is not so good! Such a stance can only be counterproductive, which means that it will be destructive. And that is our situation when we take ourselves seriously as peacemakers in the global village. A global context is the true context in which we are called upon to live; if we denied it, we would be in trouble. The fact of the matter is that we *do* deny it, and we *are* in trouble. That's bad news, and we must explore it before we can return to the good news.

How we explore it is crucial. We are Christians and we are Americans. Living in the global village calls on us to be Christians first and Americans second; indeed, that is the liberating statement of the good news. But in actuality, we are usually Americans first and Christians second; that is the burdensome reality of the bad news.

If we are to be Christians first and Americans second, what will that demand of us specifically? It will demand that we *see the world through eyes other than our own,* through the eyes of the poor and dispossessed, the eyes of the starving and despairing. And it will similarly demand that we *listen to the world through voices other than our own,* the voices of the oppressed who are despairing and angry and strident. The exercise can only be initially threatening.

Let us engage in the exercise, even so. Let us try to understand how others see our world, and, more importantly, how they see us.

Let us begin with an individual who is not a threat to readers of a volume such as this, Robert McNamara, who spent several years helping to supervise our globally destructive policy in Vietnam, and later tried to implement policies that he believed would help us to be enablers of the global village rather than destroyers. (I am not, by referring to him, endorsing the policies of the World Bank, about which most Third World Christians have grave questions. But I am saluting his intention to see the world from another perspective than the one he previously had. He who was not poor tried to listen to those who were.) As McNamara looked at what the rich nations were doing to combat the aching poverty of the rest of the world, his indictment was stern. Widespread poverty, he said, "is an open insult to the human dignity of us all . . . for we have had it in our power to do more to fight poverty and we have failed to do so" (*San Jose Mercury,* Oct. 1, 1980, p. 4a). McNamara said, in other words, that we Americans are *not* adopting a global perspective, that we are *not* concerning ourselves with human need beyond our shores, and that the little we are doing is, in his words, "disgracefully inadequate." Those are not the words of a radical fanatic on a soap box, nor are they the words of someone facing us with a machine gun and demanding that we fork over all we have. Those are the words of Robert McNamara. When he tests us on an elemental human problem, poverty, he finds us wanting.

That is a start, but only a start. It is not enough to hear

an American telling us what he hears others saying. We must hear the others' words directly. So as a second exercise, let us listen to portions of an extraordinary document, "An Open Letter to North American Christians," signed by thirteen Christians from Latin America. These signers include a Presbyterian moderator, the president of an evangelical seminary, a Baptist minister, a Methodist superintendent, a Lutheran coordinator, a Methodist and an Episcopal bishop, a Peruvian evangelical pastor, and five others whose names could not be released because of the danger in which such an act would put them. These are the voices of those who are first of all our Christian sisters and brothers, and secondly citizens of Central and South America. They claim solidarity with us in the faith we all share in Jesus Christ. And out of that solidarity in the *good* news, they speak words that, initially at least, can only be heard by us as *bad* news. They put us to the test: is our commitment to the good news strong enough to enable us truly to hear, and heed, the bad news that comes hard on its heels?

Our Brothers and Sisters:
  . . . Can you comprehend the reason for our preoccupation with your election [of a new president]? It is due to the fact that we are trapped in the same system —with the exception of Cuba. We all move within one economic-political-military complex, in which one finds committed fabulous interests of financial groups which dominate the life of your country and the Creole oligarchies of our Latin American nations. Both groups, more allied today than ever, have held back time after time, the great transformations that our people need and desperately demand.
  If we still had some doubt regarding this sad and painful "Pan-American" reality, the scandalous inter-

vention of the United States in the installation and maintenance of military regimes in Guatemala, Nicaragua, Brazil, Paraguay, Bolivia, etc.: the revelation of the activities of the ITT and other North American business in Chile; the resounding case of Watergate; the discoveries about the CIA and other agencies of penetration and espionage in our countries; the shameful Panamanian enclave with its military training centers which our Christian and Latin American consciences cannot tolerate any longer. . . . All this and much more has been opening our eyes to a reality that . . . has demolished the image of "the great democracy of the North," which we have been taught to admire. . . .

Today, we Latin Americans are discovering that, apart from our own weaknesses and sins, not a few of our misfortunes, miseries and frustrations flow from and are perpetuated within a system that produces substantial benefits for your country, but which goes on swallowing us more and more in oppression, in impotence, in death. In a few words: your precious "American way of life," the opulence of your magnates, your economic and military domination, feeds in no small proportion on the blood which gushes—according to one of our most brilliant essayists—"from the open veins of Latin America."

The writers describe the tyrannical regimes of terror in Latin America that are supported by the United States, the methods of electronic torture learned from us, the "silent genocide," i.e., starvation, to which economic exploitation condemns their people, the prisons, the corpses, after which they comment:

All this, our brothers and sisters, is carried out in the name of "democracy," in the name of "Western Christian civilization," on the backs of our people, and with the benediction and the support of your govern-

ment, of your armed forces, without which our dictators could not maintain themselves in power for much
time.

Friends and fellow Christians, it is time that you
realize that our continent is becoming one gigantic
prison, and in some regions, one vast cemetery, that
human rights, the grand guidelines of the gospel, are
becoming a dead letter, without force. And all this in
order to maintain a system, a structure of dependency
that benefits the mighty privileged persons of a minority of your land and of our land, at the expense of
the poor millions who are increasing throughout the
width and breadth of the continent. . . . This letter
seeks to be an anguished, fervent call to your conscience and to your responsibility as Christians.

The writers then spell out what they feel to be our
responsibility as Christians:

If in the past you felt it to be your apostolic duty to
send us missionaries and economic resources, today
the frontier of your witness and Christian solidarity is
within your own country. The conscious, intelligent,
and responsible use of your vote; the appeal to your
representatives in Congress; the application of pressure by various means on your authorities, can contribute to changing the course of our governments
toward paths of greater justice and brotherhood, or to
accentuate a colonialist and oppressive policy over
our peoples. In this sense you must ask yourselves if
you will or will not be "your brother's keeper" in
these lands of America, from which the blood of millions of Abels is clamoring to heaven.

We, between tears and groans, are interceding for
you, in order that you may respond with faithfulness
to the historic responsibility which, as citizens of one
of the great contemporary powers and as disciples of
Jesus Christ, it falls on you to assume. . . .

Fraternally, in Christ the Lord

How do we respond to such powerful and passionate words: With anger? Resentment? Shame? Acquiescence? Defensiveness? Openness? Wondering what our spouses would think? Feeling that religion and politics are being mixed in ways they should not be? Questioning whether or not it was all a bit of Marxist propaganda? As a disturbing statement of how things really are?

It is this kind of exercise to which the task of "peacemaking in the global village" must open us. For we North Americans do not see ourselves as predators, as oppressors, as those whose comforts are purchased at the cost of the destruction of others. Yet that is the way we are perceived by others, even by our fellow Christians. Do we have the courage to look at ourselves through their eyes?

It is not enough to respond, "Oh, come now, it can't be that bad. Why, I was in Buenos Aires only last summer, and *I* didn't see any torture." We must start with the premise that the truth is being spoken: people are hurting.

But the message is not only *"We* are hurting"; it is *"You* are hurting us." That people might be hurting—of course that is possible. But that we are hurting them—that is surely too much! But that is what they tell us; that our government, our policies, our business, our CIA, our police academies, are not only hurting but destroying them. They ask us to stop hurting and destroying them. And they suggest some very concrete things that we, in our elections, ought to do, since we have the privilege (denied to most of them) of using an electoral process to hold our public officials accountable, and to put them out of office if they do not render satisfactory accountability.

To hear the "Open Letter" with openness is to begin to see the world with eyes other than our own, to have taken a step toward Christian maturity.

A third exercise in trying to act as peacemaker in the

global village is to look at things we think we understand,
but about which living in the global village forces us to
think differently. An important example is the question of
violence, and we have some lessons to learn from one of
the great Christians of our time, Dom Helder Câmara, the
Roman Catholic archbishop of Recife, Brazil. Dom Helder
is a revolutionary, but he feels that revolution must be
achieved nonviolently. He has therefore thought a lot
about violence. In a little book, *The Spiral of Violence,* he
distinguished three kinds of violence. Violence No. 1 he
calls *injustice,* the state of things when children are starving to death although there is food enough for all, the
situation when innocent people are rounded up and imprisoned without trial, the reality that families freeze to
death in tenement buildings because the landlord won't
turn on the heat for those who are behind in their rent.
This is often called "institutionalized violence," "structural violence," or "the violence of the status quo." Sometimes it is called "invisible violence," because it is invisible
to all save its victims. If we have trouble understanding
how such things can be called "violence," that says more
about the narrowness of our perspective than about the
breadth of the definition.

When Violence No. 1, injustice, gets too bad, Dom
Helder continues, Violence No. 2, or *revolt,* breaks out.
The blacks in Watts or Newark reach a breaking point and
a riot starts; those who are hungry in Detroit become so
desperate that they lash out at the building or person
nearest to hand; the blacks in Soweto become outraged
and march.

When such things happen, those in authority respond
with Violence No. 3, or *repression.* The National Guard,
the police, the Army, are brought to the scene to stop the

revolt, to restore law and order, to ensure that the status quo returns.

This only increases the injustice, so that we are back to Violence No. 1, uglier still this time, ugly enough to provoke a worse outbreak of revolt, Violence No. 2, which will call for even heavier-handed repression, Violence No. 3, which will multiply the injustice, Violence No. 1—and so on and so on. Truly a spiral of violence.

How are we to break the spiral? *Our* answer is usually that when a riot breaks out, or a revolt starts, we must, of course as peacemakers, "stop the violence." When violence becomes visible and physical, we move to suppress it. But, says Dom Helder, such action comes too late. The only place at which the spiral can be broken is by dealing with Violence No. 1, the unjust structures of the society that produce what the signers of the "Open Letter to North American Christians" call "silent genocide," the ongoing violations of human personhood that silently, but devastatingly and relentlessly, destroy. Only by doing away with the unjust structures can we cope with violence and make peace in the global village.

I believe Dom Helder is right. Most North Americans, I have discovered, do not. But I believe he is describing reality. There need not be a mugging, a stabbing, a shooting, a rape, for violence to occur. Violence can happen silently. If a parent is forced out of work, and if his or her children starve to death, violence has been done to those children (as well as to the parent); the cause of the violence is the system of social relationships that decrees that the parent shall not work or receive bread. What needs to be curbed is not the power of the parent to lash out in outrage, but the power of the structures to dehumanize the parent and destroy the children—whether the structures are evil governments, churches in collusion with evil governments, businesses that make profits out of human exploitation, or political parties that worry only about those with influence.

If we really intend to become peacemakers in the global village, we must face the unpleasant fact that *the structures that benefit us frequently destroy others.* The police protect me; but the police can be a terror to an innocent black teenager who is mistakenly taken to the precinct station and worked over for a crime he did not commit. The courts protect my constitutional rights, and if I violate them, the courts will give me a fair trial because I can afford a good lawyer and can answer reasonably well under cross-examination before a jury largely composed of people from my own social class. But a Chicano in the central valley in California almost certainly cannot afford a good lawyer, and may not be able to respond well under cross-examination in a language that is not his or her own, before a jury composed mainly of Anglos. In such a case, the Chicano becomes the victim of injustice rather than the recipient of justice.

All this forces me to acknowledge that I, because of my privileged position, either cannot or do not see the world as it really is. I see it *as it looks from my position of privilege,* which is the position of about 1 percent of the human family. And I must be forced, painful as the process is, to see it from a different perspective.

In sum, there really *is* some bad news. Not only are we reluctant to see the world through eyes other than our own, but when we gird up our psyches and try to do so, we are the recipients of a devastating indictment. So the bad news is doubly compounded.

How are we going to deal with that? Will we be immobilized? Guilt-ridden? Angry? Defensive? Will we turn it off with pejorative terms like "communistic" or "maso-chistic" or (perhaps the most effectively patronizing word) "exaggerated"?

Having heard the bad news, let us return again to *the good news*. We discover that it will not cancel out the bad news. It will not make it go away. It will not dull its impact. But the good news will give us a context in which we can begin to confront the bad news. We can deal positively with the impact of the bad news only *if we have a higher and deeper loyalty than the partial loyalties that are so roundly challenged by the bad news*. The bad news hits us most devastatingly to the degree that we define our-selves primarily as Americans or whites or middle-class church types. There is no getting around it: if our final loyalty is to *America,* of course we will resist the notion that our nation is a predator; if our final loyalty is to *our white skin,* of course we will resist the notion that whites have been ripping off nonwhites; if our final loyalty is to *our class,* of course we will resist the notion that our class is on the side of repression and destruction; if our final loyalty is to *the institutional church,* of course we will resist the notion that it is deeply complicit in the evil deeds that darken our world today.

Such loyalties are too parochial, too partial. They must be shattered, for they in turn are shattering people every-where. What can keep us going is the reality that there already exists—in this spot and that, in remnant form—the global community to which we must be committed, wit-nessing to "the God who is above all other gods" like nation and race, and who has called us into being as a servant community that is united across all divisions.

Every now and then this community surfaces, fragmen-tarily, tremblingly, but sometimes very courageously. We see it, here and there, and realize that we too are part of

an amazing network that might be called "God's under-
ground." We sense this when we listen to a Latin American like Beatriz Couch, or derive hope from a Martin
Luther King, or affirm a Pope John, or receive an "Open
Letter to North American Christians," or hear Beyers
Naudé saying "no" to the South African government, or
have our political complacency challenged by a Mother
Teresa, or confront the countless, nameless ones, whether
in South Korea, or Santiago, or Bangalore, or Concepción,
or Chimbote, or Tokyo, who put themselves on the line in
ways we have never come close to doing. We discover that
there already is a "cloud of witnesses," and that we are a
part of that band, however feeble, timid, and lacking in
courage we may be. There *is* a network, a global community that does not have to be created, since it already is.
It may be feeble, but we have a promise on high authority
that the gates of hell will not prevail against it. And it is
within that community that we can find the staying power
to hear the bad news that comes as the other side of the
good news, and even begin to change, so that out of our
grappling with the bad news we can once again hear the
good news that there is a redeeming power already at
work in the world.

To which the response may seem obvious: "Beautiful!
But I've got news for you. It's not like that in Rahway, or
Wichita, or even the Interchurch Center. It's not like that
in Second Presbyterian, or All Saints' Episcopal. . . ."

Fair enough. That may not describe any existing congre-
gation, parish, parish council, session, vestry, or string of
clergy. But it describes half a dozen people in our town or
even in our church. That's more than enough to start.
Jesus, in fact, said that two or three were sufficient. Our
task, then, is to find that handful, that remnant, and become what Dom Helder has called "the Abrahamic minor-

ity"—what we might better call "the Abraham and Sarah minority"—the little group who, like Abraham and Sarah, venture forth, at risk, not knowing where they are going, but sure that their destination is one where the builder and maker is God. Those in such a minority must find and support one another. We must hold up the limb today on which somebody else walks out, realizing that somebody else will be ready to hold it for us whenever our moment comes.

We can be islands of global commitment working for *shalom,* wholeness and peace, in a chaotic sea of those who fear global commitment, because we have each other as well as the Lord who promises to be in our midst.

That may make life hectic and even threatening. But of one thing we can be sure. It won't be dull.

II | *War and Peace*

2
MODERN WARFARE:
CHALLENGE TO PEACEMAKERS

During his brief presidency, Gerald Ford repeatedly urged us to "forget Vietnam." We have done rather well in following his advice.

Nothing could be more disastrous. Nothing could more effectively immunize us to the reality that we live in a global village than to become a nation whose major axiom is, "Let it be for us as though Vietnam had never happened." For Vietnam is where the reality of what we do covertly elsewhere in the global village was overtly acted out. Elsewhere (in places like Chile, Greece, the Philippines) we have tried to impose our will by bribery, CIA activities, economic pressure, or political manipulation. In Vietnam we tried to impose our will by bombs. It didn't work. We need to reflect on that, or we will repeat new Vietnams elsewhere—more subtly, perhaps, but just as devastatingly, even if we use greenbacks rather than Green Berets.

There is another reason we must not "forget Vietnam." For it was Vietnam that drove home the fact that we *do* live in a global village, that events far away also have implications near at hand and have a messy habit of spilling over into one another. In the early 1960's most of us were what could be called "one-issue persons." Civil rights was the symptomatic ill that, once conquered, would open the way to a new future for everybody, black and white alike. But a few people started insisting that something was also wrong in Southeast Asia. A diversionary tactic, it seemed to us; a way to avoid seeking justice for blacks at home.

We were wrong. The two issues were the same issue: *(a)* We were destroying dark-skinned people in Ben Tre and Hanoi, just as we were destroying dark-skinned people in Montgomery and Chicago. *(b)* In order to destroy dark-skinned Asians we were sending dark-skinned Americans with twice the proportional frequency we were sending white Americans. A poster frequently carried by blacks at peace rallies went: "No VIETCONG EVER CALLED ME NIGGER." Sending blacks to walk in the valley of the shadow of death wasn't only destroying their bodies. It was destroying our soul.

We need to keep alive something of the urgency of those times, lest our consciences become dulled by the ethical narcotic whose prescription reads: "Forget Vietnam." Vietnam showed us irreversibly that we live in the global village, and that we do not necessarily comport ourselves well when we make that discovery. That is something we must not forget when we consider the nature of modern warfare.

One need not be a pacifist to be concerned about the nature of modern warfare, though it helps. One need only be a concerned citizen of the global village to realize that the very nature of modern warfare jeopardizes everything for which the global village stands. It is important, therefore, to look at the issue and examine the new kinds of questions that are thrust upon us as we contemplate the possibility of future wars.

The following discussion is divided into four sections: *(a)*

Views of Warfare in the Bible and in the Church; *(b)* The "Just War"; *(c)* Characteristics of Modern Warfare; and *(d)* Resultant Questions for the Churches.

A. VIEWS OF WARFARE IN THE BIBLE AND IN THE CHURCH

There is a great deal about warfare in the writings that have nourished our Western culture, the Old and New Testaments. If anything emerges with clarity after an examination of their contents, it is that no single viewpoint dominates the great variety of writings that comprise the Jewish and Christian Scriptures. The devil, as has been pointed out many times, can quote Scripture for his purposes, and in no area of our experience, perhaps, has this been truer than in the uses to which Scripture has been put in justifying or condemning war.

We must first guard against an oversimplification that often intrudes in Christian circles, to the effect that the God of the Old Testament is a God of warfare and vengeance, while the God of the New Testament is a God of love and peace. This is one of those polemical generalizations that will not hold up under even the most superficial scrutiny. To be sure, there are bloodthirsty passages in the Old Testament—a fact that should not be surprising, considering the historical context out of which many of those passages came into being. We find the psalmist, for example, saying, "Happy shall he be who takes your little ones and dashes them against the rock!" (Ps. 137:9), and we find Saul being castigated because after a particular battle he did *not* follow the divine command to "slay all the men, women, and children of the Amalekites."

But if there are passages like these, there are also passages that witness to the surpassing tenderness of God's love for all people, and the peace that God will bring. Here is the prophet Isaiah:

> They shall beat their swords into plowshares, and their spears into pruning hooks; nation shall not lift up sword against nation, neither shall they learn war any more. (Isa. 2:4; see also Micah 4:3)

Few pictures of a world at peace are more exalted than that contained later in Isaiah:

> The wolf shall dwell with the lamb, and the leopard shall lie down with the kid, and the calf and the lion and the fatling together, and a little child shall lead them. The cow and the bear shall feed; their young shall lie down together; and the lion shall eat straw like the ox. The suckling child shall play over the hole of the asp, and the weaned child shall put his hand on the adder's den. They shall not hurt nor destroy in all my holy mountain; for the earth shall be full of the knowledge of the LORD as the waters cover the sea. (Isa. 11:6–9)

Another crucial emphasis in the Old Testament is the stress on the *justice* of God, a justice that is combined with mercy. The universe has a moral character, according to the Old Testament writers, which ensures that in the end those who commit injustice will be brought low. Again and again the prophets inveigh against injustice, and when its excesses become sufficiently exacerbating, injustice is always challenged and God is found to be on the side of the oppressed. Condemnation is not reserved for those who commit violence against injustice, but for those who are the architects of the injustice that makes committing violence necessary.

In the New Testament there are various attitudes as well. John the Baptist does not tell soldiers to go AWOL; he merely urges them not to grumble about their wages.

Jesus says, "I have not come to bring peace, but a sword" (Matt. 10:34), which, even though it may be only a metaphor, is nevertheless a particularly military metaphor. He further says, "If my kingship were of this world, my servants would fight" (John 18:36). There is no clearly recorded opposition on Jesus' part to the fact that some of his disciples took swords when they went to the Garden of Gethsemane, although he told Peter, when that impetuous follower used his sword against a soldier, "All who take the sword will perish by the sword" (Matt. 26:52).

But even if we take such scattered verses as these and add to them the incident of Jesus clearing the moneychangers out of the Temple, the overall picture that emerges clearly puts the burden of proof on those who would use Jesus' life or teachings in order to justify going to war. Not only is it wrong to *kill* the enemy—even *hating* the enemy is proscribed. There is a positive command to love, and even pray for, the enemy, who may not be the subject of retaliation; if one is smitten on the cheek, the other cheek must be turned. It is not the warmakers who are blessed, but the peacemakers (see the summary of Jesus' teaching in Matthew 5–7). The prevailing viewpoint seems clear.

Even Paul, who must have had a more choleric disposition than Jesus, sounds much the same. Paul quotes the Hebrew Scriptures:

> Bless those who persecute you; bless and do not curse them. . . . Live in harmony with one another. . . . Repay no one evil for evil, but take thought for what is noble in the sight of all. If possible, so far as it depends on you, live peaceably with all. Beloved, never avenge yourselves, but leave it to the wrath of God; for it is written, "Vengeance is mine, I will repay, says the Lord." No, "if your enemy is hungry,

feed him; if he is thirsty, give him drink; for by so doing you will heap burning coals upon his head." Do not be overcome by evil, but overcome evil with good (Rom. 12:14–21).

Even with this kind of evidence, however, we cannot make a simplistic transfer of the New Testament materials to our own time. There are at least two reasons for this. First, it is undeniable that both Jesus and Paul expected an imminent end to history; they felt that God was about to intervene and establish the divine kingdom, and that the present world situation of the Christian was going to be of relatively short duration (although Paul gradually modified his views and began to deal with the church's problem of preparing for a long-term future on earth). Secondly, there is the further complication that recent New Testament studies make it more difficult to determine precisely what Jesus' own attitude was toward the "revolutionary movements" at work in his day. It is somewhat surprising to learn that one and possibly two of the twelve apostles were Zealots, members of a revolutionary group dedicated to overthrowing the Roman government by force. An extended literature has grown up around the problem of Jesus' attitude toward the Zealots; scholars such as Brandon have even suggested that there was a conspiracy of silence in the Gospels so that the early church would not get into further trouble with Rome as a politically subversive movement. The results of the investigation, however, while they challenge a simplistic identification of Jesus with pacifism, do not justify the notion that he can be transformed into an advocate of violent revolution.

Supporting the notion that Jesus bequeathed his followers a legacy of opposition to violence and warfare is the fact that, of the three basic positions on war that emerged in Christian history, the earliest was an unequivocal *pacifism.* The early Christians, who took very seriously the injunction that they were not to take up the sword, refused to serve in Roman armies for several centuries. Early literature gives ample evidence of the pacifist position of the Christian church.

Later on, when the peace and stability of the Roman Empire were threatened by the invasion of barbarians from the north, Christians began to argue that there might be times when they could be justified in waging war, if certain specified criteria were met. This position came to be called the doctrine of *the just war,* and we shall shortly examine it. A third position that emerged still later was the theory of *the holy war* or *crusade,* which involved an acceptance of whatever kind of force or violence was necessary to secure a given end, and the unquestioning participation of the Christian on the assumption that God's will was being served.

Although the latter position is seldom advanced by responsible church leaders today, it is frequently echoed in the public rhetoric of politicians—Ronald Reagan's reference to America's presence in Vietnam as a noble cause being only a single case in point. The options of pacifism and the just war, however, have persisted throughout Christian history and have increasingly influenced contemporary thinking, particularly in relation to the formulation of a position on conscientious objection to war. It will be helpful to look more closely at both of them.

B. The "Just War"

One of the most interesting developments in recent theology has been the revival of the "just war" theory. This position was developed by Augustine (in response to the circumstances cited above), given careful treatment by Thomas Aquinas in the medieval period, and further refined by the Jesuit theologian Suárez during the Counter-Reformation. It subsequently fell into disrepute largely because any war being waged by the country in which a proponent of the theory resided invariably turned out to be a "just war"—a situation that has changed only in recent years, as we shall presently see.

There are at least six criteria by reference to which a war might be denominated "just":

1. The war must be *declared by a legitimate authority*; it must not be the expression of a private grudge of an individual or group of individuals who simply decide to throw their weight around. During most of the time the just war theory has operated, "declaration by a legitimate authority" has meant declaration by a prince or sovereign head of state.

2. The war must be *carried out with a right intention*; its purpose must be to promote peace. This is simply a spelling out of the basic natural law theory in ethics, that good should be promoted and evil avoided. The war must be carried out with the intention that good shall result rather than evil, that peace and justice will follow rather than tyranny. A war cannot be just if it is waged with a wrong intention, such as the desire to secure vengeance or to satisfy lust for domination.

3. The war must be undertaken *only as a last resort*. No war can be just as long as there is *any* chance of resolving the conflict by discussion, negotiation, the employment of economic sanctions, or other means short of military action. All means for a peaceful solution must have been exhausted before resort to military force can be justified.

4. The war must be waged on the basis of *the principle of proportionality*. The relationship between ends and

means must be proportionate; i.e., there cannot be excessive destruction for the sake of even minimally desirable ends. The good to be accomplished must outweigh the evil that will be exercised in bringing about the good.

5. The war must have *a reasonable chance of success.* This is not a cynical provision but a moral consideration, for unless there is a good chance that the objective for waging war can be achieved, it is immoral to incur the damage and destruction that will result.

6. The war must be waged *with all the moderation possible.* Clear codes of conduct in time of war have emerged, embodied in internationally accepted rules of warfare endorsed by the Hague Convention, the Geneva Convention, and other such bodies. It is never legitimate to go beyond the minimal moral constraints that have been agreed upon. Wanton violence is prohibited; so is looting; so are massacres. Particular care must be taken to see that civilian noncombatants and prisoners of war are not tortured or killed. The criterion has reference not only to the actual hostilities but also to the terms of settlement at the end of the war—terms that must embody charity and justice rather than vengeance.

Father John Coleman, S.J., has noted certain important things about the application of these criteria: *(a)* The presumption in "just war" theory is always *against* war, not in favor of it. There is no attempt to glorify war or to make it seem less evil than it is. The burden of proof is always upon the one who would wage war, and *all* of the criteria must be met if the war is to be called "just." *(b)* The criteria remain operative *during* the waging of the war. A war originally undertaken for just cause could be waged so unjustly that continuing participation in it might have to be condemned. Most Christians, for example, felt that the initiation of war against Nazism was just, but many were increasingly troubled by the obliteration bombing of German cities, the imposition of unconditional surrender, and the American use of atomic weapons in Japan. Such actions increasingly called into question the justness of the Allied cause. *(c)* Since the presumption is always against war, there is a built-in presumption in support of dissent from participation in war. The principle that certain wars could be just carries with it the corollary that other wars might be unjust. It would follow that an individual could participate in a just war but not in an unjust war. Without calling oneself an absolute pacifist, one could still insist on the right to "selective conscientious objection" to a particular war if it did not meet the criteria that would allow for conscientious participation.

The above discussion offers a fairly optimistic view of the uses to which the doctrine of the just war can be put. It is therefore important to note some of the limitations of the just war theory.

One of these is that until recent times, proponents of a just war theory have invariably been able to justify any wars in which their own nations were involved, suggesting that the theory has the built-in danger of being no more than a self-serving device. A second problem is that the nations (or, in the past, the monarchs) serve as judges in their own case. Who is to say that all legitimate alternatives have been exhausted before war is declared? Presumably only the ones who have tried them out and had access to sufficient information to make intelligent decisions on the matter. Once again, self-serving rationalization can enter in. It will be remembered that in the early days of the escalation of the Vietnam War, public questioning was always countered with the insistence that only "the experts" knew enough to be able to make decisions.

The most sustained recent attack on the just war theory is offered by James Douglass, a Roman Catholic pacifist, in *The Non-Violent Cross* (Macmillan Co., 1969). While Douglass' response is directed chiefly against the particular version of the just war theory espoused by Paul Ramsey, the points he makes deserve thoughtful attention. He believes that the just war theory has too many loopholes, and as a consequence its proponents can always find a rationale for supporting war. Christians, he feels, must be so transformed that "conscience will not only be purged of the nuclear sword but reformed in the strength of the nonviolent cross." He feels that "a morally limited war has already been excluded from possibility in the Nuclear Age," and that any just war theory that can countenance nuclear warfare has demonstrated its moral bankruptcy and has, however imperceptibly, given its sanction to total war. The components of just war theory do not seem to him strong enough to withstand the pressures to support a nuclear war. The notion of "justifying" from a Christian perspective "25 million discriminately dead" (as the result of a preemptive air strike) against the prospect of "215 million indiscriminately dead" (if a major power launches an attack to which another power responds) strikes Douglass (and me) as grotesque.

I do not believe, however, that the version of the just war expounded above and the position espoused by Douglass are at a far remove from each other, even though he proceeds from an absolute pacifist position and I do not. The logic of the just war position in the nuclear age seems to me to come very close to Douglass' own position. I can come close to accepting his own statement of the terms under which a just war theory could possess moral integrity:

To preserve its own integrity in the Nuclear Age, the
just war doctrine demands of the nation the cross of
unilateral disarmament—and if the nation refuses
[which I believe it will—R.M.B.], it demands of the
individual the cross of conscientious objection. Unless
the just war doctrine can support a stand in conscience against all war in the Nuclear Age, whether it
be the savagery of counterrevolutionary warfare or
the global suicide of thermonuclear war, the doctrine
is revealed as a de facto capitulation to total war. (*The
Non-Violent Cross*, p. 171)

The point of difference comes, I believe, at whether it
is an *a priori* truth that an internal revolution, seeking to
overthrow an unjust regime, will escalate into "total war."
Vietnam is strong evidence that it may, since America's
intervention led to destruction so massive that any distinction between it and total war is a semantic subtlety surely
lost upon the Vietnamese victims. It did not, however,
lead to total war in a global sense. It is conceivable that
America may have learned a lesson from its disastrous
intervention—a lesson from which other world powers
might also learn—though it will require the utmost public
vigilance to keep that lesson in mind when revolutionary
forces in some other small country threaten the stability
of American interests there.

It is not only James Douglass who sees pacifism as the
true moral possibility for our time. The witness of many
others, symbolized by the Berrigan brothers and their
friends on the "Catholic left," is indicative of what may
become an increasing commitment, particularly among
the young. Many have been pushed toward pacifism as
they have explored what it would mean to participate in
the Vietnam War, and have come to the conclusion that
participation in such a war would be morally reprehensi-
ble. Furthermore, they have come to see Vietnam not

simply as one unfortunate exaggeration of the nature of modern warfare, but as a wholly typical example of what warfare is likely to be in the future. An examination of the morality of the Vietnam War persuades them that similar standards of morality will obtain in all future wars—that moral constraints will again be eroded to the vanishing point so that the only possible reply to the demand to participate in a future war must be a resounding "no."

The position is further buttressed by the disastrous side effects of modern war. Those who say no to modern war see that a nation putting its industry, economy, and man and woman power into a war inevitably neglects using those resources to combat racism, urban blight, and unequal opportunities for education, as national priorities become increasingly distorted. They see war as a laboratory in which technicians experiment at human expense with new devices for human destruction, from napalm and white phosphorus bombs to automated battlefields. They see the mood of wartime as one that threatens the legitimacy of dissent and thereby erodes the democratic process, and they can point to any number of utterances by Johnson, Humphrey, Nixon, Agnew, Reagan, or Carter to make their point. They see Americans perturbed as white-skinned soldiers die, but increasingly unperturbed as dark-skinned soldiers and civilians die. In short, the cumulative impact of modern warfare, far from the battlefield as well as on it, only reinforces their conviction that they have passed the point of no return in relation to support of warfare.

They are, in other words, very close to the position of the early church, even though they have arrived there by a different route. Pacifism, which may once have seemed idealistic and unrealistic as a human stance, looks increasingly like the most hardheaded and realistic position imaginable. Our next topic will give further evidence for this judgment.

C. Characteristics of Modern Warfare

1. *The automated battlefield.* The nature of warfare has been fundamentally altered by the fact that much person-to-person combat is now omitted. Extraordinary technological advances mean that areas can be patrolled and defended, and that attacks on areas can be instigated, by computerized devices operated at a great distance. This is true not only of ground warfare but even more of aerial bombardment, since those dropping the bombs often never even see the target or confront in any way the human consequences of their actions. The resulting dehumanization makes the human consequences even more devastating.

2. The refinement of *antipersonnel weapons* is another by-product of technological expertise. The provisions of most international conventions outlaw the use of weapons designed to inflict cruel or unnecessary pain upon human beings, and yet these have become a common part of modern warfare. Napalm and guava bombs are only two of the most obvious examples. The continual refinement of both weapons (a more efficient napalm that cannot be scraped off human flesh, a guava bomb with plastic rather than steel pellets so that once embedded in human flesh they cannot be detected by X-ray equipment) indicates a new emphasis on the destruction of human rather than military targets and a kind of self-generating process of "improvement" that seems blind to moral consequences.

3. The *extensiveness of destruction* has reached a new magnitude. This not only involves more widespread dev-

astation from bombing attacks with conventional bombs (more tonnage was dropped on Hanoi in six days of the "Christmas bombing" than was dropped on Britain in six years of World War II) and the human destructiveness of the antipersonnel weapons referred to above. It also involves the use of defoliants, herbicides, and various gases that not only destroy forests, vegetation, and arable land but may, by their widespread use, upset the ecological balance for generations to come. We are beginning to discover that those who handled these weapons in Vietnam are now, years later, experiencing the slow but irreversible disintegration of their cellular tissues. Our nation has recently resumed the construction of instruments of chemical and germ warfare. Various nerve gases may produce genetic malformations in future generations. The ever-present threat of an escalation to nuclear weapons is a further example of the potential extensiveness of destruction.

4. The *breakdown of clear distinctions between civilian and combatant* means that even so-called "limited wars" are total in their immediate impact. Such distinctions are obviously *technically* impossible in aerial bombardment. In guerrilla warfare the distinction is *ideologically* obscured as well; anyone on the "other side" is assumed to be giving help—the farmer by growing food for the soldier, the mother by caring for the family and releasing the father to fight, and so forth. Extensive and indiscriminate killing of "civilians" can thus be justified as reducing the overall capability of the enemy to retaliate.

5. Modern warfare is further characterized by an increasing *erosion of moral constraint*, not only on the part of those who participate directly but also on the part of those who set policies. The civilian massacres at My Lai by

American soldiers merely symbolize hundreds of other such incidents in the Vietnam War for which the civilian policy makers in Washington were as morally and legally responsible as Lieut. Calley. The disturbing fact is not only that such incidents take place but that they are condoned or even defended as necessary and inevitable. While instances of unnecessary brutality abound in the history of warfare, it can be argued that there are more of them now with less qualms of collective conscience than in the past. That all parties in the Vietnam War violated the agreed-upon rules for international warfare seems to bother no one. If we do not retain at least minimal moral constraints, it is but a short step to saying that "anything goes" in order to win.

6. The magnitude and efficiency of our weaponry make it increasingly attractive to *use military means to solve political problems.* Our lavish support of military dictatorships by arms, Green Berets, and counterinsurgency training is only one example. We are faced with an increasing temptation to use massive military might as a shortcut for, and avoidance of, painstaking negotiations.

7. A consequence of the above is *the increasing power of the military in the political and economic decision-making process.* This is most simply illustrated by the massive proportion of the national budget that goes to the military. It is also illustrated by the fact that the military gets not only the financial but also, apparently, the moral priority. Programs for racial minorities, the handicapped, the mentally ill, the disadvantaged, are cut to the bone or eliminated altogether on the pretext of avoiding a raise in taxes or "welfare-statism," while the military budget increases dramatically. The principle of "cutting out the fat" applies to education budgets but not to the Pentagon.

Reputable economists argue that thirty million dollars could be cut from the military budget without destroying any defense capability. It is a "new" situation when the Pentagon's assessment of military needs determines whether or not urban rehabilitation or programs for minority groups are going to be funded.

Business is also increasingly beholden to the military. The unquestioned willingness of large corporations to manufacture antipersonnel weapons is but a single disturbing example. One might argue the importance of producing, say, precision bombing instruments that could pinpoint and limit destruction, and claim a moral obligation to produce such weapons. But it is hard to see the transferability of the argument to weapons designed merely to inflict physical pain and human bodily suffering. That transfer, however, is constantly being made. During the Vietnam War some corporations publicly professed a willingness to manufacture whatever they were told to manufacture, and did so. The modern battlefield thus becomes a laboratory for experimentation in new methods of warfare, using human beings for experimentation, with the cooperation of the civilian sector.

8. Domestically, one of the serious issues intensified by modern warfare has been *the concentration of enormous (and, many feel, unconstitutional) power in the hands of the executive branch of government.* Without a declaration of war, one President sent 500,000 troops overseas without approval of Congress, while another President— answerable to no one—invaded two neutral countries, mined harbors and ordered bombing attacks of unprecedented intensity. The fact that the imbalance of constitutionally defined powers was extended during Watergate far beyond powers claimed by the President as "Comman-

der in Chief of the Armed Forces" only underlines the seriousness of the problem for the health of a democratic society.

9. We are also confronted with an increasing need for governments engaging in modern warfare to *curtail the right of dissent*. We saw this very clearly during the Vietnam War, and the direction of all of the draft legislation President Carter introduced after the Iran crisis in 1980 was to cut back rights of conscientious objection even *below* those provisions that were achieved, after years of struggle, under the previous Selective Service Act. The initial draft registration of nineteen- and twenty-year-olds in the summer of 1980 contained no provision whatever for the statement of conscientious objection. We face possible new repetitions of very narrow provisions for conscientious objection, limited to absolute pacifists from "peace churches," without rights for humanists of conscience, and involving once again the arrest, jailing, and intimidation of public dissenters, such as we witnessed under the administrations of Lyndon Johnson and Richard Nixon. Those Presidents, as well as their Vice Presidents, Humphrey and Agnew, virtually equated dissent with disloyalty and treason, and extraordinary efforts were made by the Justice Department and the FBI to use the judicial process for intimidation. We forget such events at our peril.

10. In a time when global thinking is imperative, the intensity of modern warfare exacerbates the tendency to *think in terms of individual nations rather than of the global village*. This has been manifested in many ways: *(a)* the systematic disregard of all international conventions to which we and other nations are signatories (the Hague and Geneva conventions, the principles of Nuremberg, etc.); *(b)* the willingness to take international risks of unparalleled magnitude in defiance of the rights and

wishes of other nations (the mining of Haiphong harbor as the unilateral closing of an international waterway, and the aborted attempt to rescue the Iranian hostages at just the moment when other nations were beginning to take seriously the need for economic sanctions); *(c)* the willingness to pursue military goals without regard for either the inhabitants or the perpetrators (the use of defoliants, destruction of forests, arable land, etc., in Southeast Asia in ways lethal to troops using the defoliants as well as those on whom they were dropped); *(d)* the unwillingness to respond to international pressures (the isolation and unavailability of President Nixon during the "Christmas bombings" in Hanoi, the discarding of warnings that admitting the Shah of Iran to the United States would have baleful consequences). It is the accumulation of such instances of a nationalistically oriented mentality in the era of the global family that makes the waging of modern war so much more potentially threatening to the entire race than ever before.

11. *The increasing willingness of policymakers to engage in deliberate public deception.* This is a bipartisan activity: the Pentagon Papers illustrated deliberate deception in the Johnson administration, and the press liaison men of the Nixon administration did the same. (Several days after the foreign press reported the destruction of the Bach Mai hospital in Hanoi, the Pentagon press agent was still insisting that we had not bombed it.) The record of the last fifteen years is full of military officials falsifying reports of enemy strength to get bigger appropriations, news "blackout" of events in which our troops were involved, increasing manipulation of the media to create impressions contrary to fact, and so on. The ease with which this technique was spread to nonmilitary matters was only one of the lessons of the Watergate scandal.

D. Resultant Questions for the Churches

How are we to respond to the realities noted in the above three sections? What role should the churches be playing? What new questions must be asked? What follows is an initial posing of such questions.

1. The magnitude of modern warfare ought to force Christians and the churches to face the fundamental question: *Have we not come to a time when war is so utterly out of hand that it must be unambiguously repudiated?* The question is not going to be answered in the affirmative by many church bodies, at least not yet, but it must be faced, and many individuals within those churches are beginning to answer it in the affirmative. We are at least at a point where the churches must insist that the burden of proof is *always* on those who would wage war rather than on those who refuse to do so. Historically, that has never been the conviction of more than a few "peace churches." May not the time have come when it must be urged as the normative Christian position, particularly for mainline denominations?

2. Is there not a new obligation to *reexamine the traditional criteria for a "just war"?* Late in the day, these began to have impact in discussion about the Vietnam War, particularly within the Roman Catholic community, and on the assumption that future wars might at least begin in ways comparable to the Vietnam War, the criteria might be increasingly important in forming the Christian conscience. Do any of the traditional criteria apply today? What new criteria are needed in view of the new dimensions of modern warfare discussed above? How can legitimate criteria be introduced into the public discussion? If the churches do not take a pacifist stance, but at

least refuse giving uncritical blessing to future wars, they must develop something akin to a doctrine of just—and unjust—wars. Helpful moral guidance might be forthcoming from such study, especially in the light of the fact that it is difficult if not impossible to make a case for a "just" war today on the basis of the traditional criteria.

3. What is *the true nature of the nuclear threat?* Sample questions: Is it likely that any nation will be foolhardy enough to use nuclear weapons? Conversely, is it not likely that any nation could decide to initiate a "preemptive first strike"? How do we balance over thirty years of "total abstinence" against increasing nuclear stockpiling and the likelihood that someone in a moment of desperation might make a unilateral decision? Can we bank on the fact that future wars will be "limited" rather than total? Is there a significant moral difference between dropping one nuclear bomb and dropping thousands of "conventional" bombs that can produce equal or greater destruction? (These matters are pursued further in the next chapter, "Reversing the Arms Race.")

4. How can churches deal with *the nationalistic obsessiveness* that is a significant contributing factor to war and (even more tragically) to prolongation of war? Surely this is one place where the church is, in principle, well equipped to respond, since it is an international and not a national organization, and since the very nature of its ultimate allegiance compels it to choose Christ rather than Caesar when the issue is joined. There are ways to spell out creatively the implications of "You shall have no other gods before me," and churches could draw upon supranationalistic priorities that have characterized the church in the past at its best. This theme has ramifications in the assignment of moral priorities: should we consider the defense budget more important than urban renewal? Can

leaders of a modern nation be guilty of "war crimes"?

5. Does not the church have an obligation to give *mas-sive support to the right of dissent* and to be, whenever necessary, the practitioner of dissent as well as the advocate and supporter of the right of dissent for others? Most Christians would approve of that principle in general terms, and one sign of the vitality of the American churches will be their willingness to work on behalf of those who may in the future refuse to fight for reasons of conscience.

6. What should be *the role of the church in its ministry to those in the military?* Can the necessary moral witness about the nature of modern warfare be made by servants of the church who are in the uniform of, and are being paid by, the government that wages such warfare? The lack of moral outcry about the Vietnam War by military chaplains, in the face of the extraordinary outcry elsewhere, puts the burden of proof on those who claim that significant moral protest can come from church leaders already within the military. It was not chaplains who deserted for reasons of conscience, or engaged in public unwillingness to obey orders, or ferreted out the truth about My Lai.

It is not fair, however, to use the military chaplaincy as a scapegoat, for the same kinds of moral issues are raised for those who ministered to the civilian makers of antipersonnel weapons as are raised for those who ministered to the soldiers who used them. Must we not now see "civilians" simply as "military out of uniform" when involved in war production? Perhaps we should not, in principle, disengage the issue of ministry to the military from ministry to a culture that is dominated by the military. During the Vietnam years, for example, cabinet officials such as William Rogers and Melvin Laird confronted the same moral issues as those on the field of battle who had to implement decisions made in the State Department and the Pentagon. Indeed, the moral accountability of civilian officials who issue orders may be a good deal higher than that of the military personnel who "follow orders."

7. How do we deal with *the new "impersonality" of modern warfare?* The pilots and bombardiers almost uniformly report that they never thought about what they were doing above Vietnam, since they saw themselves as pushing buttons rather than incinerating people. Should they have to think about it now? Should the church force them to confront the issue of the indiscriminate destruction that resulted from B-52 raids? Could such persons endure to confront what it is humanly like to be on the ground rather than in the air, and still fly their missions? Is there a message here of judgment—and forgiveness— that is being evaded? Are we getting to the point where the decisions about what kind of war to fight in which place are being made by computers rather than by human beings? Is this an underscored instance of an increasing subservience to machines that reduces us to machines also?

8. Is *the draft* an appropriate national vehicle for military preparedness? The shift after Vietnam to a volunteer army was clearly not taken irreversibly, and the decision by President Carter to ask Congress to reinstitute registration (and a probable draft) indicates that the issue is not going to go away. Is a military draft consistent with a democratic society? Does having a volunteer army in fact mean that such an army will be composed mainly of members of minority groups who cannot find gainful employment elsewhere in our "democratic" society? Will not a readily available manpower pool (even possibly augmented in the future by womanpower) make it easier for

a country to start deploying troops short of actual declared war, and recapitulate the situation that delivered half a million troops to Vietnam without any declaration of war or even Congressional approval?

9. Finally, how can the church deal with *the formation and maintenance of conscience*, not only of those in uniform but also of those in situations beholden to men in uniform? We saw in Vietnam the almost total erosion of moral constraints in the field of battle; we saw the same thing in the policymakers who developed tactics that necessitated "free-fire zones," forcible deportation of villagers, indiscriminate use of antipersonnel weapons, and —the great contribution of Vietnam to the annals of modern "civilized" warfare—destroying cities in order to save them.

What emerges here most clearly is the issue of *idolatry* —whether of the nation, the command of the superior officer, or in acceptance of the dictum that "the President knows best." This is an issue about which the churches have considerable resources on which to draw, though the resources have not been marshaled with anything like the consistency we now need. While we must be careful not to draw facile analogies between Germany in the 1930's and the United States in the 1980's, there are lessons to be learned from the former experience— even more important in our case, since the destruction of rights of conscience is more subtle in our case. We will probably not confront such blatant invasions of personal integrity as storm troopers, pogroms, death camps, and the like—though all those are repeatable possibilities in a situation where people relax their guard—but we do, daily, confront assaults on the right of a free press, challenges to critical television reporting, distortion of news by governmental manipulators, in ways that prepare us

to be a nation of sheep. The churches have a crucial responsibility in this area not only for their own survival
but for the well-being of the entire society in which they
are situated.

3
REVERSING THE ARMS RACE

What resources are available to deal with the spectacle of an arms escalation that gets increasingly out of hand? An initial handle is provided by an anonymous seventeenth-century writer: "I had rather see coming toward me a whole regiment with drawn swords, than one lone Calvinist convinced that he is doing the will of God."

That comment illustrates both the greatness and the demonic quality of Calvinism, and, by extension, all other theological positions. There is a demonic quality, because it is easy for people to determine what *they* want to do, and then find ways to persuade themselves that it is also the will of God. Any bad idea is worse when it can claim divine sanction. The "Kill a Commie for Christ" syndrome is far more deeply ingrained in our culture than we care to admit. For the sake of "Christian civilization," and in opposition to "atheistic godless communism," we do demonic things—like building 30,000 nuclear weapons—and call it the doing of God's will. So there is a demonry in the statement.

But there is also a greatness in it. At their best, Calvinists and others have been marvelously freed up by the thought that in acting they might be doing God's will. If we feel that it is God's will for us to do *x,* then we can be liberated from fear of failing, granted courage to take risks, freed up to attempt what we might not otherwise attempt, since we can be sure that the ultimate disposition of what we do is in God's hands. It may be that our lot will be to fail, so that others can learn from our failure; or it may be that we will do more than we might otherwise have attempted, because we believe that we are not alone and that God will empower us in meeting an otherwise overwhelming challenge.

It is, needless to say, the glory rather than the demonry that we need to emulate today. We face seemingly insuperable barriers and overwhelming odds in even thinking about reversing the arms race. So powerful are the forces arrayed against us that we are almost tempted to throw in the towel before beginning. But if we can believe that it is the will of God that God's children live in peace, rather than dying in war—a proposition that is not particularly difficult to entertain—then perhaps we can be energized to see ourselves as instruments for the carrying out of that will. And if we can so see ourselves, it is conceivable that we might rise to new heights. The odds are mammoth, but we can commit ourselves with a little more abandon and courage if we believe that the divine intention is fulfilled in working for a reversal of the arms race rather than an escalation of it.

With that overall framework, let us examine some theological considerations appropriate to such a concern.

1. Our first consideration has to do with *how we think theologically* about the issue. A theological Copernican revolution is under way. Not too long ago one would have begun with a few doctrines (God, Christ, church, human nature, sin, salvation), spelled them out briefly as "timeless truths," and then "applied" them to the matter at hand. I have become disenchanted with that approach. Theol-

ogy is not a collection of "timeless truths" just waiting to be applied. Theology grows out of the situations in which we find ourselves, forged as we act, wrestle, contend, fail, and sometimes win modest victories. In Gustavo Gutiérrez' phrase, theology is "the second act," commitment being the first act; it is "critical reflection on praxis," as we bring our critical faculties into play in the light of a gospel that also came out of conflict situations. So we are called upon to *start with the situation,* and see what kind of theological conclusions it forces on us.

Let us give it a try. How does one describe our human situation in terms of the arms race? The answer is distressingly clear: it is one of madness. In the name of trying to be "realistic," we have lost touch with reality. We have the military capability to kill everybody in the world twelve times, so we want to increase that killing capacity to fifteen or sixteen times. We have 30,000 nuclear weapons in our stockpile, and Russia has at least half that many, and yet we accede without quibbling when military men, whose way of life depends on it, tell us that we need still more nuclear weapons. We are told that building more weapons will make our situation safer, when each weapon we build actually makes it more precarious. We talk about the death of 140 million people in a preemptive first strike as an "acceptable" loss of life.

One need not elaborate the script. The possibilities for irony, for satire, for tragedy, are legion. There is no logic to it. It is simply and utterly mad. We can reduce it to one proposition: *the more weapons we build, the less secure we are; therefore we will build more weapons.*

This is madness. It is madness in the sense of being utterly out of touch with reality, unable to discern what is going on, unable to read the signs of the times, a kind of madness we could call "clinical madness." People who think this way (even more, people who *act* this way) should be locked up to save the world from them. But instead, they are the ones who run the Pentagon, the Congress, the multinational corporations, and the White House. There is a bit of this madness in all of us, whenever we reason from a narrowly defined view of "national security."

So our new theological starting point is the madness, the insanity, of the world around us.

2. How do we respond to that in the name of the gospel? We might propose pitting sanity against madness, if we could figure out what it meant to be sane in such a world. But a better response might be to contrast the "clinical madness" of the people who are making the decisions, with what Abraham Heschel has called "moral madness," the madness of the prophets. The prophets, as Heschel has reminded us, were frequently called "mad" because they refused to accept the state of things around them as normative. They were very angular: Amos never even won third prize in the Bethel Chamber of Commerce Annual Award for Promising Young Dressers of Sycamore Trees; Jeremiah wasn't ever asked back to preach a second time after his candidating sermon. They proposed new allegiances, fresh ways of looking at life, challenges to those in authority. They were called mad because *they did not conform to the norms of their society*.

Without taking on the prophetic mantle too pretentiously, we can affirm that in relation to the arms race, we have a similar theological task: to refuse to conform to the norms of *our* society.

We begin with the premise that the people running things have got it all wrong: their priorities are skewed, their visions of the future are incorrect, and their remedies, rather than being remedies, are recipes for disaster.

We continue with a decision that we are not going to buy into a way of looking at the future that says, "The more precarious we make it, the better it will be for everybody." We need the brashness to affirm that whatever we know, or do not know, about God's will, we know at least that it is not God's will that, having created this earth, God is now urging earth's children to destroy it and one another. Against the "clinical madness" of the Pentagon mentality, we must pose the "moral madness" of a prophetic tradition that challenges the principalities and powers of this world and claims to be answerable to someone or something else, however hard it may be to get absolutely clear direction signals. At the very least, we know that *some* directions are wrong, and that whatever the new direction is to be, it will be a different direction from the one on which we are currently embarked. Let us opt for "moral madness."

3. Part of the "clinical madness" of the arms race is that *human community* is denied, or is defined in terms that exclude almost every community except our own. We are willing to destroy other communities, such as the Russian or the Chinese, to "save" our own community, even though an attempt to destroy them will almost inevitably lead to the destruction of much of our own community as well. In such situations we can talk about competing forces or ideological opponents, but we cannot really talk about community.

What would be an appropriate response to the sort of human expression of madness that says that "we have to destroy community in order to save it"? A concept of *global* community is the only possible alternative. And, as we noted in the initial chapter, we do not need to create a global community; it already exists. It exists in the church, or, more precisely, in a *remnant* of the church that says, "We will define who we are, not first as Americans, or white, or rich, or middle class, but as members of the global family." If the crying need is for a sense of global community, we can engage in at least modest rejoicing, for that community is already around. It surfaces every now and then, reminding us that *we are not, even now, alone.* We are part of a cloud of witnesses, a communion of saints. When we feel alone, or weak, or lacking in courage, we can remember that we have a model we can embody: we are a "preview of coming attractions" (one of my favorite definitions of the church), in relation to which other people might see enough of what the "coming attraction" is, however fractured by sin, to want to become part of such a community themselves. We must never undersell what that means for us now, and what it could mean for others in the future.

4. The notion of community is related to another point; as we look at the horrors around us we have to *rethink our understanding of the human person.* What does the present situation tell us about who we really are? Perhaps the most important thing it tells us is that we are *fearful,* so fearful that we have gradually surrendered to a concept of "national security" that purports to relieve us of fear, but at the cost of turning power and decision-making authority over to others. Whom do we really trust to make those decisions for us? We trust the military people, the ones who love the bomb, who produce the charts at the Senate hearings, who have the hard sell ("do what we say or the Russians will destroy us"), who wrap their authority in a uniformed aura that makes it well-nigh unchallengeable.

So we let the military people make the decisions that control our domestic and foreign policy. The old-fashioned way was to have our domestic and foreign policy decisions control our military posture—a much healthier way. Not only do we trust the military people; we and they place our final trust in the computers, and the human factor is increasingly subordinated. Military minds are increasingly formed by what the computer feeds into them. Again, the old-fashioned way was to have the computers informed by the information we fed into them—a much healthier way also.

So we are in process of surrendering our ability to control our destiny. We are turning it over to generals and admirals who in turn salute the real Chief of Staff, a box with the letters "IBM" written across its chest.

What a travesty of human nature! What a betrayal! This is what the Bible calls idolatry; giving absolute allegiance to that which merits only conditional allegiance, whether it is a man with gold braid on his sleeve or a box disgorging printouts from its belly. To these we must surrender our freedom and our capacity for decision-making?

What is called for here is the beginning of *naysaying*, challenging the power of such authorities, acknowledging that any God worthy of the name and worthy of allegiance will not be the God of one nation or race or class, but of all. The sooner we begin to explore ways to topple the idols and return our allegiance to the proper source, the better the prospect for human survival.

To serve the Pentagon or the computer (if there is a difference) is not to achieve freedom; it is to attain the ultimate in bondage, since it is an allegiance that leads to death. To serve the God of Abraham and Isaac, of Sarah and Leah, and the God of Jesus Christ is, in a paradoxical way, to find freedom rather than bondage, to be free to opt for life instead of death, for choice instead of puppetry, for a future instead of a past that nobody will be able to remember because nobody will be left to take note of it. Put another way, this means a new set of priorities that can

challenge the development of the neutron bomb, a creation of modern technology that destroys people but not
buildings. In the logic of the neutron bomb, things are
more ultimate than people: once we get rid of the people,
the buildings will be all right because they don't harm one
another.

5. What does the situation tell us about the dark side of
human nature that we call *sin?* Sin does not seem to be a
rebellion lodged only in individuals; we are not on a collision course with disaster because a few evil people are
maneuvering us in that direction. No, we are on a collision
course with disaster because the "good" people have become impotent; power has gone out of their hands, not to
evil people, but to a set of structures that virtually have a
life of their own that we can no longer control. Sin is
systemic. It is not just writ small in the human heart
(though there is enough and more right there); it is writ
large in social structures that surround us and increasingly
engulf us. There is a logical and technological inevitability
in these structures that goes like this: if something is bigger, it is better. If it is better, we must have it. If it can be
built, we will build it. If not, the computers will help us
learn how to do so.

Needless to say, the decision-makers in the Pentagon
are not sitting around saying: "Let's see now, how can we
disfigure babies? How can we burn elderly people? How
can we mutilate the best of our youth?" And yet their
corporate decisions and actions inevitably lead in such
directions. There is a power of evil abroad, so menacing
and so threatening that we can hardly contemplate it. This
is not true only in relation to nuclear war. It is true in
relation to the fact that children starve by the thousands,
not because evil people will it, but because decent people
are so much in complicity with structures of corporate evil

that, without wanting to do so, they are consenting unto the starvings, the burnings, the mutilations.

If the sin is somehow lodged in the structures, at least part of the remedy will have to be the redemption of the structures, which may first mean their overthrow. Nobody likes to hear that kind of talk, particularly churchgoers, most of whom work for those same structures and support those in the pulpits who occasionally challenge the structures. Just to realize that inevitable involvement would be a large part of the battle in beginning to think about alternate structures. Part of the task is also to stop scapegoating —to realize that it is cheap evasion to blame it all on the Russians, or the communists, or the Cubans, or the Chinese, or even (as these paragraphs come perilously close to doing) the Pentagon, as though all responsibility could be placed in front of a single door.

6. Where is God in such a scenario? Theologically, we need to take seriously what our forebears called divine *judgment*. This doesn't mean resurrecting a vengeful deity hurling thunderbolts at recalcitrants. It does mean affirming that somehow, in the long run if not the short, we live in a moral universe, that we can get away with evil for just so long, and that there then comes some kind of retribution, some kind of judgment.

That's not the easiest thing to affirm these days; the Nazi holocaust makes it hard not only to believe in a loving God but also to believe in a judging God, since many people rightly ask where God was in those holocaust years, when so badly needed. Equations of God and moral judgment are not easy in the best of circumstances, and they are complicated even more in relation to the arms race, because by the time judgment is finally visited on the miscreants it may be so devastatingly efficient that nobody will be left to notice it and profit from the lesson.

At least we can affirm that a kind of ghastly logic is illustrated by our increasing reliance on arms to save us: *the more dependent we become on arms, the less secure we are.* The ratio is inverse. That is a secular statement about the judgment of God. To put ultimate reliance on the wrong thing is to have all reliances threatened; to trust the wrong God is to have mistrust at the heart of everything else. To let loose radioactive wastes is to guarantee cellular destruction to our descendants. There is a negative moral logic at work, and it goes: *We may think we're getting away with it, but we're not.*

7. That's quite a bit of denunciation. But, as Paulo Freire reminds us, there must be not only denunciation but also *annunciation.* There is not only darkness, there is light, or we would not even know we were in the darkness. Here and there people offer new visions.

So we must engage in some vision-tasting. We must look for those small signs that people are in protest against the Pentagon mentality, and join forces with them. We must exalt every word or deed that suggests that the human family is more important than just the American family, or that the white family is not worth preserving at the expense of the black family. We must be that group of people who will announce alternatives, who will use the word "conversion" not only to talk about changes in one's soul but to talk about job conversion, factory conversion, energy conversion—all kinds of conversions or instances of "turning around." There is plenty of expertise to accomplish such conversions in our culture, if we are willing to tap it and mobilize it.

To say this is not to offer some merely humanistic alternative devoid of theological content. It is to affirm such things as the following:

—Whatever else the Kingdom of God may be, it is a reality in which people dwell together in peace because there is justice.

—Wherever else the Kingdom of God may be, it must be here on earth, and our job is to be instruments through which its creation can be manifested more fully.

—Whoever else Jesus Christ may be, he is one who lives among us, sides with the poor and destitute, affirms their worth at whatever cost to himself.

So we don't need "one lone Calvinist" anymore; we need people who will say:

—We've only gotten a glimpse of the vision, but we'll work with what we've got.

—We've not been all the way up the mountaintop with Brother Martin, but we've seen far enough to realize that things don't need to be the way they are.

—We may not know all the right directions, but we know some of the wrong ones, and we can say good-by to them.

—If we're truly going to confront the arms race, at least we've got to examine socialism and not let it be the scare word of the generation; at least we've got to challenge capitalism and not let it be the sacrosanct word of the generation; at least we've got to see what might be some new mixes of the two that don't escalate into Stalinism, but also don't escalate into the mind-blowing profits that are clutched by the few at the cost of hope, and even life, to the many.

All of this can be brought to a new focus by casting it in *the mood of Advent.* In the Christian year, Advent is a time of waiting: there is a rumor around that things might get better, that somebody might come and help to make them better. There are wisps of hope here and there. Somebody is coming. What will he be like? Who knows for sure? We have welcomed him many times, but he wears different garb in different ages. So we can't even be sure ahead of time; the one we wait for may not be the one who comes. What our society wants vindicated may be challenged by his coming. In a war-bent world, who can really welcome one known as the Prince of Peace? In a society that oppresses millions of its own members, who can welcome a liberator who talks about freeing the captives and bringing liberty to the oppressed? In a time when power is the name of the game, who is going to look twice at the epitome of sheer powerlessness—a baby?

The Advent mood, in other words, counsels us to *be ready for surprises*, since the one who comes may be other than the one we anticipate. We want a sense of mystery, in which it is appropriate to "let all mortal flesh keep silence"? Very well; but perhaps he will come in such a way that "the very stones will cry out" if we do not. We want a gentle savior? Very well; but perhaps he will come as a liberator, as one of the Advent hymns points out:

> He comes to break oppression,
> To set the captive free,
> To take away transgression,
> And rule in equity.

> He comes with succor speedy
> To those who suffer wrong;
> To help the poor and needy,
> And bid the weak be strong.

Nobody ever knows how the liberator will come next time, so every time we have to be ready for surprises. And that means something very important. It means that *we can look ahead with hope.* It means that we are not locked into a situation devoid of the possibility of change. It means that "more of the same" can never be the last word, and that we get the shock of our lives each time the Advent hope is fulfilled. It means that despair is toppled from top billing. It means that things can be different. It means that we can be energized into taking on even the toughest job of our time—reversing the arms race—not because we have all the expertise (though we need all we can get); not because we have the most numbers (though the more like-minded people we can gather, the better our case will be); not because victory is sure (though we must live as though it were, and at the same time work like hell to make it so—which I offer as a modern definition of the theological doctrine of sanctification).

We can run with perseverance the race that is set before us, we can rejoice in the cloud of witnesses, we can avoid succumbing to despair, because we are convinced that in our universe there is someone with whom we can side, who also works for peace and justice rather than war and destruction. If we are Jews, we can look for a first coming; if Christians, for a second, but we can look together because all that really separates us at this point is that we have different timetables. We can find staying power, not because we generate it out of our own juices, but because deep in our hearts we are convinced that decency and hope and fresh beginnings have an eternal grounding, and that to be working for their realization is to be doing the work that is most noble, most fulfilling, and most bound to strike a responsive chord in other hearts as well.

III | Interdependence in the Global Village

4

TO THE POOR, VIOLENCE IS AN EMPTY STOMACH

Living in the global village is by no means adequately described when we have tried to take account of the massive reality of warfare in our recent history. We make the disturbing discovery that all issues are interrelated—from hunger to violence to warfare to the arms race to human rights to foreign policy to our own assessment of who we are. No one of these can be fully understood apart from the others, so citizens who work for peace in the global village have the responsibility to try to see them in relationship to one another.

The insidious rhetoric of recent political platforms and campaigners has tried to move us in the opposite direction. They have tried to sell us on the necessity for American "independence" in the 1980's and to do whatever is necessary to maintain undiminished our American way of life, no matter what happens elsewhere.

A vision of this kind of "independence" is both immoral and impossible. Even if it could be achieved, it would be immoral to assume that a few have the right to all they want while the rest perish, populating a lavish oasis in an ever-widening desert of want and destitution. But the vision is also impossible; those in the desert are simply not going to sit by peaceably and let those in the oasis get

richer and richer, and fatter and fatter, while the rest
starve. Clearly hunger is related to violence.

Dom Helder Câmara's analysis of violence, outlined in
Chapter 1, applies fully to American society. If we are
concerned about violence in the United States, we must
direct our attention to injustice—to the violence of the
status quo, to the structural and institutional violence
through which America abuses so many of its citizens. This
will, of course, require a deeper understanding of violence
than we North Americans have possessed. We need con-
stant reminders that violence occurs not only when a person is mugged, raped, or shot, but also when minority
people are denied job opportunities, when blacks are
harassed by the police, when Chicano workers are denied
collective bargaining rights, when women are given unequal pay, when homosexuals are denied jobs, and when
the impoverished are given inferior schooling. Such injus-
tices destroy people and, as such, are acts of violence. They
destroy peace as well.

Pope John put it very well: "If you want peace, work for
justice." But to do that work, the American majority—
those who are white, middle-class, and comfortably situated—must begin to see themselves and the world
through eyes other than their own. As beneficiaries of the
status quo, most North Americans believe that their society and the world are just—but believing something does
not make it so. One person's peace is another's violence;
justice for one people may entail violence against another.
To the poor, violence is an empty stomach.

Much of the discussion about food now centers on the
image of "lifeboat ethics." According to this image, the
rich nations have their own lifeboats, full up but sea-
worthy, while the poor nations are in badly provisioned
boats that are sinking. So the poor are quite naturally

trying to climb into the lifeboats of the rich. The rich, so the theory goes, are justified in beating off the poor, because if the poor get on board, the lifeboats of the rich will not only run short of provisions but will be swamped to boot, so that everybody will perish. Better that some survive than none—particularly if those who survive under this arrangement happen to be ourselves.

The image assumes that the lifeboats of the rich are already full to bursting. An image more descriptive of the reality of the situation would suggest that the rich are in fact on a large yacht, if not a luxury liner, and that there is actually plenty of food and space on board, so that the rich, even if they decided to keep the first-class quarters to themselves, could afford to let the poor on board.

But there is an even more useful image, the image of our planet as a spaceship. Its value is that it stresses the element of *interdependence,* at a time when many people are unrealistically calling for independence. On a spaceship, everybody is in the act together. No one can be ignored. The entire mission is threatened if there is a mutiny among the crew.

How are the resources aboard this spaceship being divided? Theodore Hesburgh has put it this way: "Take the view of the earth from the moon that reduces the size of our spacecraft earth. Instead of 3.6 billion people, difficult to manage, think of a crew of five persons, each representing a segment of humanity. The first person representing us and our world, mostly Judeo-Christian, white, Western, affluent, has the use of 80 percent of the available life resources and amenities aboard our spacecraft. The other four crew members must share the 20 percent that is left."

That, in itself, is a statistic that Fr. Hesburgh rightly describes as "iniquitous and unjust." But, he goes on, the situation "is still deteriorating. Our crew member is in-

creasing his share to 90 percent at the moment, leaving
2½ percent for each of the other crew members."

It is frequently the case in our hard and stern world that
those who talk about "morality" are written off as naive or
sentimental or unrealistic. But in the case at hand, who is
unrealistic? The one who says that those with 90 percent
of the resources must share them with those who have
only 10 percent? Or the one who says that those with 90
percent of the resources should hold on to them, come
what may? Love and justice would, of course, indicate
sharing as the only appropriate stance. But even the most
hard-nosed kind of "realism" indicates the same thing.
Here is a case, in other words, where a moral concern
coincides with the realistic self-interest of the entire
human family. And since nations do not usually act for
moral or altruistic reasons, but out of a sense of national
self-interest, there is at least the possibility that the rich
nations might realize that they are presently pursuing a
collision course with disaster. So let us reject the notion
that a concern to share food resources is "unrealistic." It
is the only realism left.

There is an immediate need to share, made apparent in
statistics so stark that they can hardly be internalized:
15,000 people starving to death every day, two thirds of
the human family going to bed hungry every night. We
cannot ignore those realities, since they are not statistics
but people. We cannot write them off while we make
long-range plans to feed the planet more adequately in
the future by new social structures. The immediate needs
must be met by stopgap methods, and this is legitimate
and imperative, so long as we remember that they *are*
stopgap, and that they are not solving the problem but
only locating it. The experts have many suggestions for
doing this—stopgap, transitional, and long range. It is true

that there is inordinate wastage of food in "developed" countries, that we often destroy food to keep prices up, that fertilizer would be of more use on the fields in India than on cemeteries in America, that grain is more important in the stomachs of people than in the stomachs of cattle being fed the grain merely to produce a better quality of beef. But it is a long way from knowing something is true to doing something about it.

In the face of that, almost any gesture, however token, can be a useful *first* step, so long as it is seen for that and no more. Deliberately cutting down on our own food consumption, for example, will not actually help starving people very much, but it may be a consciousness-raising experience that can make us more alert to the problem. The occasional public "fasts" that many organizations sponsor may provide a few meals for people elsewhere; but their main value is to help those who engage in the fasts to experience, even if only to a small degree, what it means to be hungry.

One thing that must eventuate from such efforts at consciousness-raising is a determination to deal with *immediate* worldwide hunger by the massive transfer of food from areas of affluence to areas of need. This can be done by private humanitarian agencies, by government grants and consignments, and by the pooling of the resources of international agencies. Assuming that there are food resources to do this (and there are plenty of grounds for making that assumption), the difficulties with this step are at least two: (*a*) the relief is only temporary and does not solve the problem, and (*b*) exploitation becomes easy, e.g., feed "friends" and ignore "enemies." In the immortal and immoral words of former Secretary of Agriculture Earl Butz, food becomes a "weapon."

Such immediate aid to starving areas is crucial from any

moral (and, as has been argued, realistic) point of view—
provided it is not assumed that this answers the problem,
for it does not. It only defines the problem. *The problem
is not hunger. The problem is injustice.* The problem is
that we have a system in which the haves increasingly
benefit lavishly, at the expense of the have-nots. It is built
into the system that the rich get richer while the poor get
poorer. So food, however much it is immediately needed
simply for sustaining life, must not be confused with a
solution to the problem of hunger.

Here is where seeing the interrelatedness of all our global problems becomes so important. For we cannot isolate
food as a problem to be dealt with in isolation. Everything
else impinges upon it; it impinges on everything else.

Example: In a post-Vietnam situation in Southeast Asia
we have made some attempts, not very effective, to feed
starving peoples. To the degree that we do so, that is good.
But we need always to see the degree to which we created
the food shortages and the refugees. We napalmed their
villages, we defoliated their forests, we rendered their rice
fields unplowable. So the problem of hunger is exacerbated by the problem of *militarism.*

Example: we have food stamps for American blacks who
don't have enough money to pay regular prices. It is good
that they get food, but *we* have created the conditions that
make it impossible for them to attain an adequate earning
capacity. We have segregated their housing, denied them
first-rate schooling, and thereby effectively closed off all
kinds of jobs to them. So the problem of hunger is exacerbated by the problem of *racism.*

Example: there are thousands of people in Chile who
are starving because inflation rates have soared out of sight
and the Chilean government will do nothing about it. But
that government, the military *junta* of Pinochet, seized

power and remains in power with American connivance and help; our country helps to sponsor starvation on the outskirts of Valparaiso and Concepción. So the problem of hunger is exacerbated by the ugly reality of *imperialism.*

The recital could continue. We will not have "solved" the one problem until we have "solved" the other problems, and vice versa. Which means that we will never adequately "solve" the overall human problem of survival and humane possibilities on this planet. We will always be within a certain number of days of world starvation should there be a worldwide crop failure. We will always have to cope with the human tendency to say, "I want mine, to hell with you." We will always have to cope with the temptation described by T. S. Eliot, of "dreaming of systems so perfect that no one will need to be good."

But the immensity of the problem must not lead to immobilization of purpose. There are viable proposals for coping with immediate needs. Long-range proposals are less easy to come by, but obviously are more important if we are to draw the human family together. We cannot make it with a system based on military power as the final word, on profits for the few at the cost of misery for the many, on nation-states that seek to be "number one" at whatever cost to others.

Nor, on another level, can we make it if we insist that human need far away is unrelated to human affluence at home, if we "stonewall" against change because change is threatening and inconvenient and uncomfortable, if we insist that individual and private efforts alone can solve communal and public problems.

All of this suggests that what we most need is a combination of moral motivation and technical expertise. If motivation alone can be sentimental, expertise alone can be manipulative. Perhaps at the end of the day our American choice will not be whether we *can* give the help needed (surely we can), but whether we *will* (perhaps we will not). For any significant coping with world hunger will be very threatening to American power and prestige, let alone the American standard of living. These are not matters that should be glossed over. They require (both in motivation and expertise) the presence of the churches and synagogues, along with that of politicians, sociologists, political scientists, and even theologians.

This is why concern with hunger will inevitably involve us in politics, and in a kind of political decision-making in which the ingredient of love must always be related to the question of justice—which may, for our day, turn out to be the crucial relationship. Aristotle long ago defined justice as "giving every person his [or her] due." We can improve on that by extending the definition to read "giving every child his or her due," since that is where much of the terrible tragedy of hunger is located. Providing food won't be the end of the road leading to wholeness and peace in the global village. But it is certainly close to the beginning. United States citizens are a global minority, constituting just 6 percent of the world's population while consuming 40 percent of its resources. Clearly, then, our world is one in which a tiny minority controls an inordinate share of power and wealth. I do not believe that the deprived majority of the human family will let such a state of affairs go unchallenged much longer. Realistically, I foresee a future that includes drastic pressure for reallocating the world's goods and resources.

Wow!

That is where the issue of violence once again becomes a central concern for North Americans who long for peace. Will the United States continue a global course based on "Violence No. 1" (injustice) until "Violence No. 2" (revolt) becomes inevitable and America is forced to respond with "Violence No. 3" (repression)?

Will we North Americans continue to believe that only overt acts of rebellion by the deprived are violent? Or will we begin to see that, from the perspective of the dispossessed, the world is already filled with the violence of injustice? How else must the world seem to the poor who send their children to bed hungry knowing full well that most children in North America have more than enough to eat?

It is my rather desperate hope that our nation still retains enough compassion to realize that we cannot go on piling up goods and power regardless of what happens to the dispossessed. As John Kennedy once remarked, "Those who make peaceful revolution impossible will make violent revolution inevitable."

Unless we reflect seriously on those words, that aphorism could become our epitaph.

5
CHRISTIAN RESPONSIBILITY IN HUMAN RIGHTS

Sometimes the issues of peacemaking in the global village seem so overwhelming, or so far away, that we feel frustrated and defeated before we even begin to consider them. What difference can *we* make in a world of such massive structures, such vast distances, such complex and interconnected problems?

There is no formula for collapsing the complexity or negating the massiveness. But there are places where we can begin, right now, to "make a difference," clear-cut starting points that will gradually move us into other interconnected areas with their more complex problems. One such starting point is "human rights." Whether the issue is the right to speak one's mind, or the right to have sufficient food, or the right to take political stands without being imprisoned or tortured, we know that such rights are basic, and that their denial jeopardizes not only the persons mistreated, but the very possibility of peace in the world. For there is no true peace when human rights are denied. So wherever that denial is present—across the street, across the city, in Alabama or Afghanistan, in Iowa or Iran, in Chicago or Chile—there is a task for the peacemakers. That task is the restoration of human rights.

A few years ago, writing on "Christian Responsibility in

Human Rights" would have been much simpler: one would have set forth some "theological principles" as part of a clear and unchanging Christian heritage, and then derived from them certain conclusions about human rights that could have been offered as special and possibly unique Christian insights. Two things militate against doing it that way anymore.

One of these was briefly alluded to in Chapter 3, "Reversing the Arms Race." It is the recognition—made clear by such "troublers of our [theological] peace" as Gustavo Gutiérrez—that truth, and especially the truth of the gospel, does not consist in abstract or disembodied concepts; it is forged out of engagement and struggle in specific situations, because it is dynamic rather than static. We do not arrive at truths and then "apply" them—we commit ourselves to struggle and carve out our appropriation of truth in that situation, from being "in the midst," which is where the Bible tells us God is to be found.

A second reason for not deducing conclusions about human rights exclusively from previously established theological norms is that such an enterprise can easily lead to theological cheating. Concern for human rights is not an exclusive prerogative of Christians; we may not claim that only in the light of theological or Biblical insights can people arrive at a responsible position on this matter. We need a little theological modesty at this point. Many who have never heard the gospel preached have a commitment to human rights that puts our own to shame.

WIDELY SHARED CONVICTIONS

So let us begin with some observations about human rights that all sorts of people share. Such an approach represents a theology characteristic of the Pastoral Constitution *Gaudium et Spes* of Vatican II, with its consistent theme that "we must hear the voice of God in the voice of the times," and the Biblical recognition that (as Isaiah 10 reminds us) God can work through the pagan Assyrian to proclaim and exhibit the divine will, when the people of God harden their hearts or stuff their ears with theological wax.

Concern for human rights is thus pretheological or at least paratheological. One need not be a theologian, a Biblicist, a Christian, or even, in the conventional meaning of the word, a "religious" person, to be concerned about human rights and their widespread denial. Rather than being threatened by this fact, we ought to rejoice in it, grateful that we can join hands with others far beyond our enfeebled and often dispirited Christian band. The United Nations Declaration on Human Rights is a good example of such concern. It is neither a "Christian" nor an avowedly "religious" document; it rather self-consciously seeks to avoid such adjectival charges. But we must certainly affirm with it that the rights it enunciates are to be guaranteed to all—the right to life, liberty, and security; protection from slavery and torture; equality before the law; protection from arbitrary arrest, detention, or exile; freedom of movement, the right to marry, to own property; freedom of thought, conscience, and religion; freedom to hold opinions; freedom of peaceful assembly; freedom to vote in secret; the right to social security; freedom to work, to receive equal pay for equal work, to join a union; the right to rest and leisure, to education; the right to live in a supportive social and international order; and so on.

The World Council of Churches conference on human rights at St. Pölten, Austria, in 1974 itemized six rights: the right to life, which includes protection from unjust political and economic systems; the right to a cultural identity; the right to participate in the decision-making process of one's community; the right to dissent; the right to personal dignity; the right freely to choose a faith and a religion.

With different nuances, other declarations would affirm similar agendas. There are clearly some things on which most rational people are agreed, even though different contexts may produce different emphases. This matter of context deserves brief examination since it frequently leads to misunderstanding. In our Western, democratic, capitalist countries, for example, we have tended to put particular stress on *individual* human rights—the right of protest, of dissent, freedom of speech, of movement, and so on. These have been, and remain, a precious part of our heritage. But in many other parts of the world, more stress is put on *social* human rights for all—the right to food, clothing, shelter, education, medical care, and so on. These latter rights are the ones we need to take more seriously in our own context today, since our culture has de facto tended to say that such things were not rights but privileges, available only to those who could afford to pay for them. Different societies tend to stress one of these sets of concerns and to slight the other—if we in the West have championed individual human rights above social human rights, it can be argued that elsewhere, when social human rights are championed, individual human rights may be in danger of being subordinated. In the worst situations neither set of rights is taken seriously—a reality (as we often need to remind ourselves) that can obtain under *both* rightist and leftist regimes.

So part of our own task is to get beyond the frenetic fear that concern for social human rights is "socialistic" in the pejorative meaning of that word, i.e., un-American. I think it is patently arguable, for example, that a baby born in

Cuba today under the Castro regime has a better chance
for a humane life than such a baby would have had under
the Batista regime, or would have today in Chile under the
Pinochet regime. Yet we have opposed Castro for over
twenty years and have supported, virtually sponsored,
Pinochet during and since his illegal seizure of power.

So it is clear that Christians have no corner on concern
for human rights. Furthermore, we Christians have
burned more than our share of witches, heretics, and
other deviants, whose human rights were denied and
whose tortures were arranged in the name of the Bible by
God-fearing men (one time when the retention of sexist
language is probably appropriate).

A BIBLICAL PERSPECTIVE

In the light of what we observe about the human scene
today—that this is a time of gross violation of human rights
and also a time when many people are rallying around the
need to defend human rights, often at great cost—we can
ask: what can we affirm that might bring further emphases
into the discussion and the action? Here are some reinforc-
ing emphases out of the Christian gospel:

1. One of the most important things we can affirm theologically and Biblically for an understanding of human
rights is the conviction that *every person is made in God's
image*. This says many things:

It says that each person is unique and precious, and the
one who is unique and precious may not be tortured,
starved, left without shelter, denied a chance to develop
the fullest capabilities, and so on.

It says further that what is a right for anyone must be a
right for everyone. If *our* children should not be denied
milk, neither should children in Nicaragua, and as long as

we supported the Somoza regime (almost forty years) we were denying the image of God in Nicaraguan children.

It says once again that to reflect the divine image is also to share, in ways appropriate to the creature, in the creative properties of the Creator. If God is creator, and we are molded in God's image, then being co-creators is part of the definition of who we are, called to bring the divine intention to fulfillment rather than to thwart it. And if that divine intention is love, then whatever thwarts love is to be condemned, whatever fosters love is to be affirmed. It should not be hard to draw some conclusions about what that means in the area of human rights.

2. As Reinhold Niebuhr once remarked, the one empirically verifiable Christian doctrine is the doctrine of *sin*. Particularly when we reflect on violations of human rights, we are made aware of the pervasiveness of human sin. Human behavior may shock us, but there is an important sense in which it ought never to surprise us—we should always be aware that human beings can stoop to unprecedented depths of depravity, and that when we see such activity in another we must acknowledge that it mirrors possibilities to which we ourselves could stoop. The reality of sin can keep us alert to anticipate possible abuses of human rights in even the best-run human societies (such as, presumably, our own), and to seek ways to forestall the ease with which violators of human rights can get away with it.

This is part of the corruption of the best in us, not simply an italicizing of the worst. We are wrong to call torturers "bestial." As Dostoevsky pointed out long ago, that is an insult to the beasts. So if we reflect on the interrelationship between our world and our faith, we will recognize that there always need to be social structures that will deny to individuals the chance to abuse their power, and there always need to be individuals who will deny to structures the chance to abuse their power.

To sum up points 1 and 2: If a belief in the *imago dei* means that everyone must be invested with infinite worth, a belief in sin means that no one can be invested with infinite trust.

3. It is always dangerous to concentrate the Biblical message in one concept or emphasis, but at different times in Christian history different themes have properly been stressed: grace and nature in the Middle Ages, justification by faith in the era of the Reformation, sin in the 1940's. Today the rallying theme that has emerged is *liberation:* Jesus came to bring liberation to the captives, freedom to the oppressed, good news to the poor. It is hard to fault liberation as a central Biblical concern. So let us take it seriously. If liberation is meant for one, it is meant for all. To be free, to be liberated, means more in the Biblical understanding than just to be liberated from personal guilt or private sin. It must also mean to be liberated from structures of oppression, bondage, and evil—what the Bible calls "the yoke of the oppressor." It is not the full message of the gospel that one has "found Christ" if one's child is still starving—even more, if someone else's child is still starving. Concern for liberation is the theological side of a coin that says on the reverse side, "human rights," but human rights defined in ways that get to the heart of the social, corporate dimensions of human existence and challenge the structures—whether political, economic, sociological, or ecclesiological—that deny full humanity to people. We usually overlook the fact that in Jesus' parable of the last judgment (Matthew 25), it is the *nations* that are held accountable for failing to feed the hungry, clothe the naked, and minister to the sick. Biblical faith denies us the luxury of retreating into the private arena of individual

rights for the relatively privileged; it demands social rights for the poor.

4. To talk about *God* today is difficult for many people. Let us observe that the arena in which human rights are talked about—oppressed peoples, demeaned individuals, the "wretched of the earth"—is the only arena in which the *Biblical* God can really be talked about or observed or responded to or known. There is a bias in the Bible toward the poor, as those among whom God dwells in a special way. It is with victims that God is working, i.e., with the Israelites in Egypt, or Babylon, or Palestine. When God becomes flesh it is as one of the *'am ha'aretz,* the people of the land. The God of whom we speak and to whom we pray is a God who has identified with those who suffer. As we look at the world today, we should have no difficulty affirming that the God of the Bible is with the tortured rather than the torturer; with the one who says "no" to Pinochet rather than the one who says "yes"; with the one who is in jail for political reasons rather than the one who does the jailing; with Steve Biko rather than John Vorster; with those who are hungry rather than those who are stuffed. Our understanding of God, our commitment to God, will be nurtured not by aloofness from partisan struggle, not by disengagement, but by partisanship, by involvement, since God is partisan and involved. To affirm torture, or Pinochet, or Vorster, or to be indifferent to world hunger, is "practical atheism," a denial of the God of the Bible.

5. Other areas of Biblical and theological concern could be adduced. The *church,* as the recipient of grace and as the community of those trying to embody the Jesus story themselves, must be a servant church, a remnant church identified with those in need, a protagonist of human rights. The *sacraments,* which show forth a broken body

and shed blood, can be seen as stern reminders that those nourished thereby must commit themselves to see that no more bodies are broken, and no more blood is shed, either in prison cells or through the "silent genocide" fostered by indifference to the "least of these" God's children.

FURTHER NEEDS

Having started with our situation and moved to a Biblical perspective, let us now move back to our situation in the light of that Biblical perspective. Here are a few things we need to take seriously in a new way:

1. We need to develop a *fresh capacity for anger.* The issue is not hatred but anger, outrage, of the sort that characterized Amos, Jeremiah, Isaiah, and Jesus in the face of injustice. We should have been more outraged not only by the details of Steve Biko's murder in a South African jail but also by the fact that, even in the face of the incontrovertible evidence, the South African government exonerated all parties from responsibility for his death. We should be further outraged by the reality that for every Steve Biko we know about, there are hundreds, thousands, in South Africa and elsewhere that we do not know about who suffer the same fate. Paul's injunction, "Be ye angry, and sin not" is clearly a Biblical word for our time.

2. Let us take significant account of a new dimension in the human rights struggle—*the rights of unborn generations*—who have the right to inherit an earth not contaminated by radioactive wastes, or polluted streams, or exhausted resources for production of heat and food. The ecological issue must not be counterpoised to the human rights issue as though one had to choose between them. If "the earth is the Lord's," so are "they that dwell therein," and vice versa.

3. We must see more clearly how *our economic structures* often lead to denial rather than expression of human rights. A competitive economy breeds an attitude that renders the life of the competitor expendable; work life based solely on the profit motive inevitably justifies dehumanizing those who threaten profit; an economy based on corporations accountable to no one beyond themselves means that human rights will not be taken seriously if they interfere with corporation goals; social systems designed for pocketbooks rather than persons will end up destroying persons for the sake of pocketbooks.

4. In concern for the victims of human rights violations, let us remember that while it is important to be "the voice of the voiceless," as many church pronouncements have said, that is not enough; we must find ways *to help the voiceless gain a voice of their own.* Put another way, our task is not to do things for the poor, but to empower the poor to do things for themselves. Otherwise we end up with a paternalism that demeans those whom we mean to help; they are manipulated, objectified, denied the chance to become full and responsible persons who can create their own destinies.

5. Let us rethink the prohibition against "interfering in the affairs of another nation." Granted that it can be self-righteous always to be looking at others rather than ourselves for violations of human rights, granted that we are not to tell Switzerland what its tariff policy should be or demand that Britain change its driving rules, there nevertheless comes a point at which human concerns override national autonomy. The torture of political prisoners is clearly one of those exceptions. But perhaps the list of clear exceptions should be further extended: if children are dying of slow starvation because economic or political policies dictate that their parents shall not be granted a

living wage, that too is torture. Worse than that, it is murder, the "silent genocide" that condemns millions to die annually as long as we stay on the sidelines. Perhaps more aggressiveness is needed by us in these areas; inaction may be a worse sin than moving overzealously.

6. Finally, let us remember that there is a connection between *rights and duties.* It is a duty to intervene on behalf of the rights of others if those rights are being violated. Indeed, it is a duty to act ahead of time in such a way that violations of human rights are rendered less likely. We could engage in such preventive action by attempting to create a just society in which people will not need to torture others in order to stay in power, or to support unjust economic systems so that others will be unable to gain power. Maybe then justice *could* "roll down like waters, and righteousness like a mighty stream." That would produce a beneficent flood, requiring no ark.

IV | The American Dream and the Dream of the Church

6
SEEING AMERICA IN GLOBAL TERMS

In spite of all the hopes of the peacemakers, will the American dream become the American nightmare? The question is not rhetorical. On balance, I fear that an affirmative answer (which is bad news) is more likely than a negative one (which would be good news). I am not pleased by such a conclusion. Could it be forestalled? Could religion contribute to the forestalling, and thereby to the creation of a more attractive vision of America's future?

Our peculiar religious situation is a religious pluralism in which a large number of religious options are not only available for those who desire them but are fairly well protected from disembodiment by competing options. This is the source of both the problem and the promise of religion as a catalyst on the American scene.

On the one hand, pluralism makes things messy. There is no single, overarching vision. Adherents of mutually exclusive faith claims confuse us as they parade a variety of nostrums over the airwaves or through the press—from the power of positive thinking to warnings of an imminent Armageddon, from Southern Baptist fundamentalism to New England Unitarianism, from California cultism to Episcopalian traditionalism, from uptight forms of Protes-

tantism to freed-up forms of Catholicism. How can religion unite us when such a confusing array of options is
paraded before us, pulling us (if we respond at all) in a
dozen different directions?

On the other hand, there is something promising about
the very messiness. For worse than a penchant for disarray
would be a compulsion to tidiness—a national ethos with
an overarching vision so comprehensive that there was no
room for alternatives, alternatives being seen as divisive
threats to an order achieved at great effort and even pain.

There was a time when Protestants looked on Roman
Catholicism as harboring secret designs to become the
vehicle of just such a unified vision: there was a time
within living memory when Protestants spoke fearfully of
a future in which Catholics got to be 51 percent and took
over, abolishing public education in favor of federally sub-
sidized parochial schools, installing a hot line from the
White House to the Vatican, and other things too grim to
contemplate. What those Protestants did not understand
was that for generations they had themselves embodied
the very vision they projected with such repugnance on
their Catholic counterparts—from compulsory reading of
a Protestant version of the Scriptures in the public schools
to a long history of trying to keep Catholics out of public
office (except for such unbeatable enclaves as Irish Bos-
ton), and especially out of the White House (until an Irish
Bostonian slipped through their fingers and had the ef-
frontery not to fulfill the doomsday agenda they had
created for him).

The danger is that any single vision that is initially
merely doctrinaire shortly becomes oppressive and finally
turns ugly, no matter who propounds it, whether Catholic,
Protestant, or "other." And "other" is a not an inconsider-
able item on the American agenda. The White House

mentality that was almost accidentally liquidated by the Watergate scandal embodied a "secular" counterpart to religious absolutism. After the 1972 elections, as we now know, plans were under way to purge deviants and non-believers—the obstreperous press, unfriendly television stations, militant students. No one, whether pastor, prelate, or President, is exempt from the desire to consolidate power by neutralizing the opposition.

So on these terms pluralism is an asset. It is a protection against demagoguery. It legitimates and even glorifies dissent, making dissent possible because those in power are never quite secure enough in that power to lower the boom unequivocally on those who challenge them. So with all its problems, our pluralistic situation is one for which to be grateful. It gives all of us breathing space and elbow room, so long as we don't try to commandeer all the air or elbow everybody else off the scene.

A healthy situation. But always a precarious situation, the description of a victory never fully won. To be in the minority and yet to think oneself right is not only to decide, often legitimately, to share what is right with everyone else; to be in the minority and yet to think oneself right is sometimes also to decide, often illegitimately, that if others are wrong they should not be entitled to foist their wrongheaded errors on others (the rhetoric easily begins to flow). And this, I believe, is the real danger to peacemaking in the years ahead. As our situation grows more globally precarious, as it surely will, and since fewer and fewer nations will be willing to let us have our way in the future as we had it in the past, there will be internal attempts to regroup our national forces not only against external threats ("communism") but also against internal threats ("subversion"). Whether the threats are real or presumed will not matter much. There will be a strong demand for a united national front against both external and internal threats (which can be lumped together conveniently as "communist subversion").

The most potent ally of such forces will surely be religion. The most potent adversary of such forces might possibly be religion.

There is a theological word we have confronted earlier that describes this situation. That word is "idolatry," and it means the worship of idols. Idols, in turn, are false gods. Idolatry is not an out-of-date disease that infected only the benighted dwellers in antiquity. Nor is it confined to faraway cultures where people still literally bend the knee to the tangible object of wood or stone. On the contrary, idolatry is alive and well in the U.S.A. It is the disease of those who make the nation their god—of those who say, "The United States must remain number one at all costs"; of those who say, "If they [who can be anyone] don't agree with us, bomb the hell out of them"; of those who say, "We've given the blacks a lot; why aren't they content now?" of those who say, "Sure, we use 40 percent of the world's resources and are only 6 percent of the world's population—that's nothing to be ashamed of; it only shows we're go-getting and efficient"; of those who say, "Poor people are out of work because they're lazy."

What it adds up to is: "Don't criticize us. We've got it put together. And the only way you can put it together is to be like us. We'll tell you what to do. We'll run the show. Leave it to us. Capitulate. Because if you don't"—and the rest is said very softly—"we'll run you off the globe, and don't think we haven't got the napalm, or the B-52's, or the economic leverage, or whatever else it takes, to do it."

A nasty caricature. Surely we don't talk like that. Perhaps we don't "talk like that." But we must begin to realize that particularly in Third World countries, if we don't always "talk like that," we are widely perceived as ones who *act* like that. Ask a Vietnamese farmer whose village has been bombed and whose children have been napalmed; ask a Chilean political refugee whose attempt to establish a legally elected socialist government was brutally overthrown with clear support from United States business and governmental interests; ask an Argentinian woman whose husband has just been tortured and killed for political dissent by soldiers trained in United States police academies; ask a black South African whose future depends on revolutionary change and who has discovered that change in his country is impossible as long as American corporations continue to shore up the economy of his racist government; ask a student of political and social history who has discovered that attempts by indigenous peoples to overthrow authoritarian regimes are almost invariably opposed by the United States, which supports the unjust status quo (and all the American profits invested in it) at enormous cost to human life, human dignity, and human hope.

Now that is all bad news. It is especially bad news to those who are the victims of such policies and attitudes. The good side of the bad news would be our willingness to take a fresh look at the future in the light of such a past. If idolatry—the worship of a false god—is the problem, then worship of the true God might be a remedy. And if our particular brand of idolatry is narrow nationalism, then belief in the true God might mean belief in a God who transcends such nationalism, allegiance to whom demands a global allegiance to match it. Those are two interlocking themes. Let us explore them.

If pluralism has been domestically creative in the past, a new kind of pluralism might be globally creative in the future. We realize now that there was pluralism on the

Atlantic seaboard in 1776. It is not true that "the founding fathers had a single vision." They had a multiplicity of visions. There were Quakers and Roman Catholics, landed gentry and indentured servants, Tories and Tom Paines. But there was enough unity-in-diversity and enough trust to secure a substantial common investment in freedom that enabled them not only to survive but to look ahead in hope. Whatever the mysterious alchemy that enabled those Eastern seaboard inhabitants to work together without losing their identities, it is an analogue to what is needed today on a global scale so that we members of the entire human family can work together today without losing our identities—or our shirts.

Consider. Just as there were sovereign colonies in 1776, so there are sovereign nations today. Just as those sovereign colonies gradually discovered that they must join forces in order to survive, so we sovereign nations today are rapidly discovering that we must join forces in order to survive. Just as the sovereign colonies in 1776 faced a common enemy (focused in the name of George the Third) so we sovereign nations today face a common enemy (focused in many names: global extinction, nuclear war, ecological crisis, the revolution of rising expectations).

To respond creatively to such a situation with anything like the vision of our forefathers and foremothers would mean some amazing things: A global pluralism would allow the right of survival to socialist-oriented governments; it would acknowledge that the American standard of living is obscenely disproportionate to that of most of the rest of the world; it would affirm that the poor must be involved in the decision-making processes that affect their destiny; it would take seriously the fact that financing dictatorships abroad is too high a price to pay for luxurious creature comforts at home; it would be dedicated, in other words, to the proposition that our goal must not be independence from the concerns of others, but interdependence in the needs of others.

A noble dream. A noble, impractical, unrealistic dream, assuming that a people and a nation are about to put the concerns of other peoples and nations above their own interests and become more concerned about an amorphous and not-yet-quite-discernible "global family" than they are about their own immediate, tangible, like-minded, flesh-and-blood kinfolk. Who is kidding whom?

I see two possible responses to the charge that giving priority to the global family is utopian naiveté and unrealism. They sound very different, but in some important ways they converge.

The first is the tough-minded response, and it goes like this: "True realism for the future is not national sovereignty at all costs. That way lies disaster. It simply will not be tolerated much longer by its victims. White, rich people are a minority of the human family, although they have not yet caught up with that fact. The nonwhite, poor majority is not going to allow the white, rich minority to run the show indefinitely. The transistor radio alone has enabled people all over the world to learn that a small percentage of the human family is opulent beyond the wildest dreams of everyone else. And it only gets worse—the rich continue to get richer while the poor get poorer. Not only that—the rich get richer by exploiting the poor. And the poor are going to run out of patience. Poor nations with raw materials the rich need will begin to band together. Acts of defiance on a global scale will increase. The presently impotent hatred of the rich minority will begin to change into a powerful force determined to overthrow that rich minority. And if the rich respond the way they always have—by a show of force—they will either become brutal totalitarians with such rigid defense systems that they will gradually destroy each other as well, or they will trigger a global struggle of such mammoth physical proportions and psychic intensity as to make conventional descriptions of Armageddon sound like a Sunday school teachers' convention. No, the only 'realism' is cooperation designed to help all rather than hinder most, for the alternatives are too destructive to entertain."

Such a scenario is realistic and tough-minded, all right. It is also incredibly dreary, depicting a loveless world of people motivated by fear. And fear is never a very creative or unifying factor.

So let us examine the other scenario. If the first builds upon a recognition of the dimension of sin and self-centeredness in the human disposition ("the one empirically verifiable Christian doctrine"), the second, while not slighting that kind of realism, takes account of another side of the human disposition—what Jews and Christians have described as "the image of God." We suggested above that if worship of a false god has created our present impasse, worship of the true God might provide a way beyond the impasse. Let us, for a moment at least, take our pollsters seriously when they inform us that we still consider ourselves a "religious" people, professing some kind of belief in some kind of deity. Let us assume that the God we say we worship has at least a shadowy resemblance to the God of Jewish and Christian faith, however much the resemblance has worn thin in recent years. Rediscovery of what lies behind the shadowy remains could be a significant turning point in our life as a nation.

For whatever else we may say about the God of the Old and New Testaments, such a God is not the God only of white people, or members of the middle class, or North

Americans—not even the exclusive God of Christians and Jews. The God of the Bible is the God of all people—of Egyptians and Assyrians as well as Jews, of Africans as well as Americans, of the poor as well as the rich, of the blacks as well as the whites. In fact, if we read our Scriptures diligently enough, we will make the alarming discovery that the God described there seems to have a special predilection for the oppressed, for the down and out, for "the wretched of the earth," so that to be in rapport with such a God will mean being in rapport with "the very least" of the children of such a God.

We need to stay with that for a moment, since what initially sounds so alarming may turn out to be the very liberative key we need. To translate that concern directly to our own situation would be to say that belief in such a God would free us to see the world not only through our own eyes but also through the eyes of our victims, those who suffer for what we gain. To well-fixed upper-middle-class whites, the American dream may indeed have worked; to blacks in a city ghetto, it is a nightmare from which there seems no possible awakening. To those who find fulfillment in their jobs, our economic system is a success; to those ground down by their jobs, and to the increasing number with no jobs at all, the system is a nightmare. (Remember the bumper sticker: "If you think the system is working, ask someone who isn't.") To those here at home who love coffee, its easy availability (even amid soaring prices) is a pleasant if minor luxury they enjoy; to those overseas who grow the coffee, the wage scale is a monster of exploitation, denying minimal necessities to their children and leaving their own lives daily more desperate.

Those who commit themselves to the God who is the God of the entire global family discover that justice is an inevitable component of such commitment. To believe in the God of justice is not only to be outraged at injustice but to be energized in the doing of justice oneself. No one who claims to believe in this God can any longer entertain a parochial vision—a narrow perspective that claims that special divine favors are guaranteed to us at the expense of others. The dimensions of care and concern must be enlarged beyond one's immediate family to include the entire human family—partiality is extended neither to Jew nor Greek, male nor female, bond nor free, for all are one. . . . So, at any rate, Paul saw it within the parameters of the Christian vision which for him was not circumscribing but all-embracing.

Are we as a people ready to entertain such a vision? It is clear that if we fail to do so, we not only make the first scenario described above more likely but we also forfeit the right to claim allegiance to such a God. We become "practical atheists," those whose deeds belie their words. There would at least be honesty in such an admission, acknowledging that belief in a God who is concerned for all is too demanding, and that a tame, domesticated God is preferable: the god of the American way of life; the god who blesses free enterprise, a rising GNP, napalm when necessary, and a life of luxury for us at the cost of misery for others; a god who finally becomes indistinguishable from ourselves. Such a god, it was proposed above, is an idol. The conviction may disquiet; it will not disappear.

There is no way any longer to talk about our nation without talking about our world. The destinies of both are intertwined. There is no creative way to talk about our nation *in* our world without also talking about God. To see that in a new way is the beginning of the rejection of the nightmare, a first step toward the reaffirmation of the dream, the basis for all subsequent peacemaking.

7
THE REMNANT
WITHIN THE REMNANT

A number of years ago I took a ride on a railroad train. As the conductor came down the aisle, I saw him with pity in my eyes; he was clearly working for a doomed outfit: railroads were on the way out, and this particular railroad (situated in New England) seemed to be arriving at that destination faster than most. At the completion of the journey I mentioned my pity to a friend, who responded that he had exactly the same feeling for people who were vocationally trapped in the church. From his perspective, the church was also a doomed outfit, clearly on the way out. He could not understand why people would want to be part of an organization whose days were numbered.

There are times when all of us are tempted to accept such an analysis. Indeed, such times are not all behind us. We will face them in low moments in the future. But I am increasingly clear that the temptation must be resisted. As we look at the future of the church, and its possible contribution to peacemaking, we can feel a strange kind of excitement that one of the most important and demanding places to be for the rest of this century could be within the life of the church.

Is that anything more than whistling in the dark?

Let us back into an answer. As we look at the world

today, we can only see a world that is going to get more perplexing, complex, and threatening. It is a world in which the operative descriptive terms are likely to be terms that scare us—terms like "exploitation" and "oppression" and "outrage." In a world that can no longer afford the luxury of nationalism, there will be ever more frantic efforts to shore up nationalistic dreams and defenses. In a world that cannot endure extreme divisions between rich and poor, there will be increasing demands from the poor for a legitimate share of the world's resources, and increasing defensiveness on the part of the rich against inroads into what they—into what *we*—currently have. In the scramble for power, we who have a lot are likely to want even more, so that we can "protect ourselves" against those who have very little and are prepared to indulge in drastic measures to get some.

In the face of such a grim and relentless scenario, the imperative need, and the only effective counterforce for peace and justice, is surely some embodiment of global community. Anything less will be divisive and disruptive and destructive. There is no possible way to face our own future apart from a radically global perspective. We live in the global village and we cannot wish that fact away.

If we look for signs of unity in the global village, we immediately think of the United Nations. It is crucial that we support this one political vehicle that begins to transcend national boundaries, but we must be aware that even here the very definition of membership is nationalistic before it is global. One is a member of the UN by virtue of being a nation, one is a delegate to the UN by virtue of citizenship in a given nation; from the very start the defining terms are national rather than global.

In principle, the universities can provide models for the global village, and most of us have had some experience of that, as we have mingled with students from a diversity of national and geographical origins. But it is also true that our universities more and more are getting locked into nationalistic perspectives and structures, for reasons of financial survival if nothing more. Inordinate amounts of university budgets come either from the Defense Department, dedicated to keeping America militarily able to destroy the human family, or from state legislatures that ride herd on ideas that seem to be the least bit "un-American," or from private donors who are increasingly wary of giving money to universities that might be hospitable to the expression of so-called "radical" ideas.

Another potential symbol of global perspective, the multinational corporation, is involved in similar ambiguities. The problem here is that a very few people will increasingly be able to make decisions that drastically affect the lives of millions of people, without any clear lines of accountability to those millions of people. Furthermore, the aim of these corporations is not to enhance the situation of the oppressed but to make as large a profit as possible. Rarely, if ever, are these two concerns going to be involved in mutual reinforcement.

The point of the above comments is not so much to score points against multinational corporations or universities or the United Nations, as it is to suggest that with whatever strengths and weaknesses, they are not the sufficient vehicles through which a sense of global community—responsible to all of God's children—is going to be launched.

And it is in the need for something more than these that we can dare to turn again to the church—that weak and often divisive institution which seems so feebly to reflect what it ought to be. Even in its weakness it represents in embryo the kind of global network that is essential for the survival not only of the church but of the entire human family it is here to serve. Whatever the shortcomings of its empirical institutional life—and they are legion—the church is that community in which membership is not defined by nationality or race or sex or class or geographical location, or any of the other usual criteria for defining community. The only requisite that one must fulfill to be part of the people of God is to be a person, and to be a person who acknowledges need. Whenever the church begins to create barriers that exclude people from membership on racial, national, sexist, geographical, or class terms, it is repudiating its very nature. It is, of course, "repudiating its very nature" a good deal of the time, but it has self-correcting resources within it to work on that, in the form of prophetic minorities.

Pointing to the church as a present embodiment of the global village may seem impossibly romantic. But what is being pointed to is not an organizational structure so much as something more fundamental—a network, a remnant that tangibly exists wherever two or three persons find themselves gathered together in the name of Jesus Christ. I have had the good fortune of experiencing the reality of this network a number of times in recent years, in scattered enough places to make me sure that I am not fantasizing. To me it comes clearest in liturgy, as people from extraordinarily diverse and often divisive backgrounds gather around a common table and discover, in their allegiance to the Lord who presides at that table, a unity that does indeed shatter those other realities of diversity and division.

I have experienced this in seminary chapels where denominational, racial, and sexist lines are truly overcome; with German POW's on an American naval base in World War II; in the middle of the Pacific Ocean on the fantail of a troop transport; in East Berlin at a Eucharist

celebrated together by East and West Germans, French
and Scots, Americans and Poles; in Rome with Protestant
observers at Vatican II sharing a common cup in a Wal-
densian church; in St. Peter's, at Vatican II, where, although we were only "observers" at Mass, there was an
increasing sense of at least spiritual participation that will
sometime break down those remaining canonical barriers;
in a New York City dining room where a group of Protestants and Catholics, divided by a doctrinal discussion, sud-
denly found that the sharing of bread and wine had
brought them unbelievably close to one another; in South
Africa, where black and white shared a common cup (and
I mean exactly a "common cup," shared by all) and a
common loaf, the only public meal in that scarred land in
which they can share; in Phnom Penh, Cambodia, just two
weeks before its fall, as three Americans, a German, and
a Japanese—enemies in the previous Asian war—were together trying to embody the message of reconciliation in
a Cambodia at war with itself.

But it is not only in the symbolic oneness around the
Lord's Table that the global network is alive but also in the
things that those who gather around that table *do* together elsewhere. The same reality has been present in
America on many occasions when an issue of racial injustice or protest against an immoral war has drawn human
beings together across confessional, racial, class, sexist
lines to make a common witness of protest and outrage
and hope.

This is the stuff out of which the global vision is being
built. It desperately needs nourishing in our own land,
since we Americans will be the ones most tempted to deny
the global vision necessary for peacemaking, for fear it will
threaten our way of life, or our standard of living, or a
decently upward curving line each year on our GNP. For

we have actively denied global community and peace-making with our bombs and dollars, with our CIA, and with our policy of siding with dictators against liberation groups in so many Third World nations.

Where will we find a base from which to challenge United States denials of the global vision, to raise questions about a concept of remaining No. 1 at all costs, to encourage steps, whenever made by those in public life, that seek to move beyond our immediate self-interest to a concern for the best interests of all the human family?

That base, I believe, will be found within a community that seeks *now* to embody what clearly must finally come for all. The church *is* a global community. Let it be true of *a remnant* within the institutional structures. Let that remnant not only challenge our nation, when it is guilty of arrogance, but also challenge the church itself, when it is irrelevant, or when it acquiesces to our nation's arrogance. The church itself is already a remnant within our culture; let there be within that remnant another remnant. Our hope lies with that "remnant within the remnant," those within the church (however many or few) who will continually call the church as well as the world to account in the name of the gospel.

Jürgen Moltmann states that the church's theology has too often been a "fossil theology," doing nothing but preserving unchanged an image from the past. In reaction to that, he goes on, many contemporary churches have adopted a "chameleon theology," i.e., a theology that blends into the culture around it in such a way as to be virtually indistinguishable from it. What we need in our day, he concludes, is an "anti-chameleon theology," i.e., a theology that will speak in sharp challenge to the background against which it is set. That is another way of describing the remnant posture, which in its turn is only another way of pleading for a global perspective as a basis for peacemaking—in an era when such a perspective is increasingly challenged by the self-interest of all involved.

Is it anything but utopian folly to ask for this? It is at least clear that this *does* represent the vision of what the church has always been meant to be—that community in which there is neither Jew nor Greek, bond nor free, male nor female, black nor white, rich nor poor, since all are one in Christ Jesus. It is at least clear that the church is the community that need not have success built into its self-definition. (Christopher Fry has defined Christians as "those who can afford to fail.") A company, a corporation, a university, a nation—all these must "succeed" in order to provide a convincing *rationale* for their existence. It is not the case that the church must succeed on those kinds of terms, not as long as it takes seriously two images that were present in its beginnings and have been forgotten too often in its subsequent history—the image of "the servant community," present not for its own enhancement but for the giving of succor to those around it; and the image of "the pilgrim people," that group whose task is not to "arrive," but always to be on the march, never secure in or vindicated by its own structures, but always willing to strike those structures down and venture forth again in new ways when occasion—or the will of God—demands it.

But there is something more to be said, lest it seem as though the church is being "reduced" to another social service agency to bind up the wounds of a bleeding world.

Once again, let us back into the point. The major task of the church as the peacemaking community is not "to bind up the wounds of a bleeding world," though it may need to continue to do that simply because there are still so many open wounds. The major task of the church is

rather to be the embodiment of a creation that will make
it unnecessary for people to leave one another bleeding in
the first place. This can be called "salvation" or "liberation" or "reconciliation" or any one of a number of similar
words. It will involve ministering to the whole person and
the whole society, since piecemeal approaches will no
longer do. Even to begin to do this, the church will need
to be on the revolutionary forefront, and this will be another test of the sincerity of its global vision, since for
middle-class people who live in the comfortable, sheltered
atmosphere of white North America, it is clear that our
cues will need to come from our Christian sisters and
brothers in other parts of the world who are wrestling at
first hand with the issues of oppression and starvation and
poverty, and from black and Chicano and Asian American
and native American sisters and brothers in North America who are wrestling with those issues right on our own
doorstep. They are the ones who will forge the new
agenda for the church of the future; and it will be a measure of our own commitment to the peacemaking task of
the global community to realize that however much the
leadership in that community may have emanated from us
in the past, it is not likely to do so in the future.

　　We must learn to listen, to respond with as much openness and creativity as possible, when we are presented
with a picture of the world and of ourselves that will be
very threatening to us, since it will imply the need for
drastic changes if that world is to become a tolerable
dwelling place for the vast majority of the human family.
The insights coming from minority groups in this country,
and from the Third World, are beginning to show us what
must be the shape of both the Christian community and
the entire human community in the future. This will involve rethinking our own priorities; it will involve serious

challenges to our assumptions about America's role in the world; and the real test of our commitment to the global vision of the church will be our willingness to let the leadership come from elsewhere (as is already happening in the World Council of Churches), and to adopt the role of listener, questioner, critic, and finally participant in movements that will lead us in new, sometimes threatening, but ultimately liberating directions.

How will this come about? Is *this* anything more than whistling in the dark? It will come about in part as we engage in a new kind of social analysis, a new kind of look at our world in the light of the gospel, particularly the Biblical message of the liberation that God brings to the oppressed, but it will also come about to the degree that the same gospel gives us the fresh *resources* that enable us to cope with the kinds of changes that are initially so threatening to everything that has sustained us in the past.

This will be the church's true gift to us. We need to rediscover that the meal we share around a common table is not simply a symbol of human community, but a profound expression of the reality of the *divine*-human community through which we can be strengthened to look in directions we have heretofore feared to look, and to walk in ways we have heretofore feared to walk. We need to rediscover that the scenario for our own future is too threatening to entertain, unless that future can also be seen as God's future, unless those who venture into it can rediscover that they do not go alone, but that there is already a Companion along the path. We need to rediscover that the daily resources of forgiveness and mercy from God are essential ingredients for the task of struggling for human justice and peace against odds that, without such help, would seem impossible to overcome.

From the assurance of those convictions, we can indeed

set ourselves to the task of embodying in our lives as peacemakers the vision of a global community grounded in the conviction that God is the God of all persons, and that God has sent Jesus Christ so that all may have life and have it more abundantly—no one *ex*cepted, everyone *ac*cepted. Then perhaps we may begin to know truly for the first time what Paul meant when he said about Jesus Christ that "in him all things hold together" (Col. 1:17).

V | Questions for Discussion

The questions offered below are no more than "thought-starters," designed not only to elicit responses from members of discussion groups but also to stimulate leaders of such groups to create further questions of their own. They follow the sequence of material presented within each chapter.

1. *From Good News to Bad News to Good News*

a. What are your reactions to these statements: Raising questions about our national policies and priorities is unpatriotic. We can be critical of our government without undermining the "American way of life." Peacemaking is compatible with American security.

b. Why should we be "Christians first and Americans second"?

c. What would it mean to stop sending " . . . missionaries and economic resources" to Latin America, and to work instead for changes in the foreign policy of our government? Why do the signers of the "Open Letter to North American Christians" advocate such a proposal?

d. What are specific examples of our responsibility for

injustice and economic deprivation in Latin America and elsewhere? (For further data see Penny Lernoux, *Cry of the People,* Doubleday & Co., 1980; and Richard J. Barnet and Ronald E. Müller, *Global Reach: The Power of the Multinational Corporations,* Simon & Schuster, 1974).

e. How do you respond to Dom Helder Câmara's three-fold extension of the definition of "violence"? What does this say about the structures of our own society?

f. Where is the "global community" in which peacemaking can begin? How can we discover it?

2. *Modern Warfare: Challenge to Peacemakers*

a. Why is it wrong to "forget Vietnam"? What response should be given to the claim that it would be better to put such an episode behind us than to let it continue to divide us?

b. How did the issue of racism compound the moral dilemma of our presence in Vietnam? What lessons might there be in this for peacemaking in the future?

c. What is the cumulative impact of the Biblical material on war? What clear messages appear?

d. Debate this proposition: It would be possible to wage a "just war" in the nuclear age on the basis of the traditional criteria. What are the arguments for a pacifist option as an alternative to war?

e. What characteristics of modern warfare have the most serious consequences for civilian attitudes?

f. Which "resultant questions for the churches" (section D of this chapter) seem most pressing in your community? How could they be raised in ways that would heighten perception of the life-and-death consequences of the discussion?

3. *Reversing the Arms Race*

a. Explore the logic of the claim that our starting point in describing the world today should be "madness."

b. What is "moral madness" as a perspective from which to confront the arms race? Give some examples of "moral madness" in the world today.

c. To what extent does the adjective "fearful" truly describe the mood of people today? Your mood? What are the fears that the arms race engenders? How legitimate are they?

d. What does it mean to say that sin is "lodged in the structures of our society"? Give some examples.

e. How can visions be practical and realistic? What visions could be set against the nightmare of nuclear arms escalation?

f. How does "the mood of Advent" energize us against disillusionment and despair?

g. What would happen if we began to de-escalate our armaments before other nations did? What will happen if we do not de-escalate armaments?

4. *To the Poor, Violence Is an Empty Stomach*

a. Why is a "declaration of independence" (America going it alone) inadequate for the 1980's? Why is a "declaration of interdependence" needed?

b. Why is the image of "lifeboat ethics" wrong both descriptively and morally? If you feel the image is right, indicate why.

c. What is the significance of the image of "spaceship earth" for an approach to problems of world hunger?

d. How do moral concern and "realism" converge in dealing with inequities between rich and poor?

e. Why is a policy that concentrates only on "feeding the hungry" an example of the problem rather than the solution?

f. What is the relationship of hunger to militarism? to racism? to imperialism? What does this suggest about the nature of peacemaking?

5. *Christian Responsibility in Human Rights*

a. What are some human rights that are widely acknowledged by most people? In what kind of order would you list them? How are they related to peacemaking?

b. What is the difference between *individual* human rights and *social* human rights? Why are North Americans often fearful of the latter? Why is the distinction important?

c. What is the relationship between human rights and a belief that all persons are created in God's image? That all persons are sinners? That God exercises a "preferential option for the poor"? (See p. 21, above.)

d. What does it mean to say that "if a belief in the *imago dei* means that everyone must be invested with infinite worth, a belief in sin means that no one can be invested with infinite trust"?

e. What does it mean to say that "to affirm torture ... or to be indifferent to world hunger is 'practical atheism' "?

f. How can anger be channeled creatively in the service of human rights?

g. Why might a concern for human rights lead to a reexamination of economic structures we have taken for granted? What has this to do with peacemaking?

h. What kinds of violations of human rights might make it appropriate to "interfere" in the affairs of another nation?

6. *Seeing America in Global Terms*

a. What are the assets and liabilities for peacemaking of living in a situation of religious pluralism?

b. What is the relationship between the Biblical understanding of idolatry and believing in "my country, right or wrong"?

c. Why do other nations tend to disbelieve our rhetoric when we express concern about peace and justice for the rest of the world?

d. What comparisons can be made between the situation of the American colonies in 1776 and the situation of the nations of the world in 1976? How would these comparisons give us some clues for creative peacemaking in the 1980's?

e. What are the merits and defects of the two scenarios suggested for dealing with America's role as peacemaker in the 1980's?

7. *The Remnant Within the Remnant*

a. What kind of case can be made for the United Nations, the universities, and the multinational corporations as precursors of the global village? What are the shortcomings of such claims?

b. In what ways can the church claim to embody the role of "precursor of the global village"? What would it mean to talk of the church as the "remnant within the remnant"? Are there signs that this is more than wishful thinking?

c. What are the differences between "fossil theology," "chameleon theology," and "anti-chameleon theology"? What different attitudes would these lead to in relation to peacemaking?

d. Why is it not sufficient to define the task of the church as "binding up the wounds of a bleeding world"? What more is needed if true peacemaking is to take place?

e. What unique resources can the church offer members who are serious about peacemaking?